Building Dynamics CRM 2015 Dashboards with Power BI

Build interactive and analytical sales productivity dashboards for Dynamics CRM 2015 with Power BI

Steve Ivie

[PACKT] enterprise

PUBLISHING   professional expertise distilled

BIRMINGHAM - MUMBAI

Building Dynamics CRM 2015 Dashboards with Power BI

First published: August 2015

Production reference: 1180815

Published by Packt Publishing Ltd.
Livery Place
35 Livery Street
Birmingham B3 2PB, UK.

ISBN 978-1-78528-910-1

www.packtpub.com

Credits

Author
Steve Ivie

Reviewers
Guillermo Barker
Dave Corun
Guido Preite

Commissioning Editor
Nadeem Bagban

Acquisition Editor
Harsha Bharwani

Content Development Editor
Divij Kotian

Technical Editor
Siddhesh Ghadi

Copy Editor
Relin Hedly

Project Coordinator
Nikhil Nair

Proofreader
Safis Editing

Indexer
Monica Ajmera Mehta

Graphics
Disha Haria

Production Coordinator
Nilesh R. Mohite

Cover Work
Nilesh R. Mohite

About the Author

Steve Ivie is a Microsoft business solutions advisor and author. He is also the founder of DynShare (www.dynshare.com), a learning and discovery site focused on business productivity, social collaboration, integrated solutions, and business analytics with Dynamics CRM and Office 365.

For 15 years, Steve has been working on business technologies for industries such as finance, biopharmaceutical, healthcare, professional services, manufacturing, sports, and entertainment. He is one of the few people who have a principle-level consulting record and holds professional certifications in Dynamics CRM, Dynamics GP, SharePoint, and business intelligence. Steve is an active speaker of CRMUG and a facilitator at Microsoft Customer Immersion Experience (CIE).

As a solution architect at Tribridge, he is responsible for building and presenting customized business solutions with Microsoft Dynamics CRM and Office 365, in addition to integrating Power BI and marketing Dynamics GP, Dynamics AX, and related ISV products.

I would like to thank my wife, Jill, and my children, Kyler, Abram, and Taylin, for letting me take this small journey.

I would also like to thank Tribridge and the Dynamics CRM and BI teams for their support.

I would like to take this opportunity to thank Dwight Specht and Chris Cognetta, who were kind enough to serve as reviewers for this book. Thank you for your support and suggestions. This is a much better book because of you.

About the Reviewers

Guillermo Barker is an electrical engineer from Universidad de Chile. He is also a CRM consultant and was awarded certifications in Microsoft MCT and MAP last year.

Prior to working as an operations manager at CMetrix, Guillermo spent almost 25 years in service management with a variety of CRM platforms. This experience gave him a wide knowledge about how to design and configure the different capabilities required in implementing a Dynamics CRM and how they can impact user adoption.

Additionally, he has helped many companies with CRM and its installation, deployment, reporting, and configuration. Guillermo is also a trainer at Golden Training and Comunidad CRM (www.comunidadcrm.com). He is a frequent contributor to Comunidad CRM on the Internet and has reviewed the following books for Packt Publishing:

- *Microsoft Dynamics CRM 2011 Applications (MB2-868) Certification Guide*
- *Microsoft Dynamics CRM Customization Essentials*

You can read more about Guillermo at http://www.linkedin.com/profile/view?id=32635763&trk=tab_pro. He blogs at http://www.comunidadcrm.com/guillermobarker/.

Dave Corun is employed at Avanade Inc. in the Dynamics CRM Service department. He possesses extensive skills in ASP.NET, Silverlight, SQL Server, Microsoft Dynamics CRM, performance, and load testing. With 19 years of experience, Dave has led development teams and was the architect of several large web applications before joining Avanade. He was also a senior technical instructor at New Horizons, leveraging his extensive development experience.

Dave is recognized as a thought leader and reviews books related to Microsoft technologies for Manning Publications and Packt Publishing.

Guido Preite is a software engineer and is working with Microsoft Dynamics CRM since 2010. He has extensive experience in implementing Dynamics CRM in several industries, such as packaging, luxury goods, ground engineering, and automotive. Guido is an active member of Dynamics Community and Stack Overflow. He currently works at eCraft Oy Ab, a Finnish Microsoft Gold Certified Partner focused on ERP and CRM solutions. You can find his technical blog at http://www.crmanwers.net.

In 2015, Guido became the Dynamics CRM MVP.

I would like to thank my family and colleagues for supporting me everyday.

www.PacktPub.com

Support files, eBooks, discount offers, and more

For support files and downloads related to your book, please visit www.PacktPub.com.

Did you know that Packt offers eBook versions of every book published, with PDF and ePub files available? You can upgrade to the eBook version at www.PacktPub.com and as a print book customer, you are entitled to a discount on the eBook copy. Get in touch with us at service@packtpub.com for more details.

At www.PacktPub.com, you can also read a collection of free technical articles, sign up for a range of free newsletters and receive exclusive discounts and offers on Packt books and eBooks.

https://www2.packtpub.com/books/subscription/packtlib

Do you need instant solutions to your IT questions? PacktLib is Packt's online digital book library. Here, you can search, access, and read Packt's entire library of books.

Why subscribe?

- Fully searchable across every book published by Packt
- Copy and paste, print, and bookmark content
- On demand and accessible via a web browser

Free access for Packt account holders

If you have an account with Packt at www.PacktPub.com, you can use this to access PacktLib today and view 9 entirely free books. Simply use your login credentials for immediate access.

Instant updates on new Packt books

Get notified! Find out when new books are published by following @PacktEnterprise on Twitter or the *Packt Enterprise* Facebook page.

Table of Contents

Preface

Welcome to building dashboards with Microsoft Dynamics 2015 and Power BI. Sales teams today want information that is faster and easy to access. This is where Power BI comes in. The main goal is to give users an easy way to create their own dashboards to present information in a timely and simple-to-understand format. In this book, using Power BI, we will cover the process of building and accessing refreshable dashboards with information from Dynamics CRM and Dynamics GP.

Throughout this book, we will build, deploy, and share a dashboard that looks similar to the following screenshot:

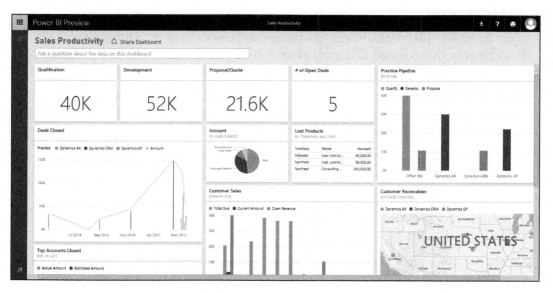

What this book covers

Chapter 1, Getting Dynamics CRM 2015 Data into Power BI, talks about how to create a Power BI site and how to connect to a Dynamics CRM 2015 organization. This chapter takes a look at the the different options on how to access Dynamics CRM 2015 data from Power BI.

Chapter 2, Organizing and Consolidating Dynamics CRM 2015 Datasets, provides information on the Mapping Dynamics CRM 2015 dataset relationships. It also shows you how to configure pivot table summaries and clean up data by formatting columns and data types.

Chapter 3, Building Summaries and Custom Calculations, discuses how to begin a sale productivity report and dashboard page. It also provides information on pipeline and sales summary information, apart from sales summary pivots and groupings with custom calculations.

Chapter 4, Improving the Look and Feel by Adding Charts, Tables, and Maps, explains how to add different visualization options to sales productivity reports and dashboards in the Power BI Designer, including tables, charts, and maps.

Chapter 5, Enhance Data Clarity Using Filters and Slicers, enables you to add interactivity, filters, and slicers to sales productivity reports and dashboards in the Power BI Designer.

Chapter 6, Adding ERP Data, offers guidelines on how to map the Dynamics CRM 2015 dataset to the external ERP data source, how to configure the sales order invoice and the payment dataset and combine it with CRM sales data in one report.

Chapter 7, Deploy and Present Reports to the Power BI Site, tells you how to publish sales productivity reports and dashboards to a secure Power BI site while configuring user access and data refresh intervals.

Chapter 8, Using Power BI Q&A to Get Results, helps users understand the Q&A functionality in Power BI and how to use it in your sales productivity dashboard.

Chapter 9, Extending the Sales Productivity Dashboard within Dynamics CRM 2015, teaches you how to embed the sale productivity Power BI Dashboard in Dynamics CRM 2015.

Chapter 10, Extend Your Dashboards to Mobile Apps, explains how to extend the sales productivity dashboard to Power BI web apps, including Microsoft Surface and Apple iPhone.

Chapter 11, Starting with the Built-in Dashboard Templates, tells you how to use the prebuilt Dynamics CRM 2015 Sale template and future Marketing and Service templates, which will be introduced soon by Microsoft.

What you need for this book

The following list shows the required software prerequisites:

- Office 365
- Dynamics CRM 2015
- Power BI Preview
- Microsoft SQL Server 2010 or higher
- Dynamics GP (optional)
- Latest web browser
- Open mind and creative attitude
- A large cup of coffee; this stuff gets addictive

Who this book is for

This book is intended to be a starting point for all salesforce users — administrators, managers, business analysts, or report writers — who are new to creating dashboards with Power BI and Dynamics CRM. It answers the questions before they are asked by providing the advanced self-service BI tools that extend the reach of Dynamics CRM reporting. With a basic knowledge of the Dynamics CRM 2015 platform, this book will help the common end user to take reporting to the next level.

Conventions

In this book, you will find a number of text styles that distinguish between different kinds of information. Here are some examples of these styles and an explanation of their meaning.

Code words in text, database table names, folder names, filenames, file extensions, pathnames, dummy URLs, user input, and Twitter handles are shown as follows: "We can include other contexts through the use of the `include` directive."

A block of code is set as follows:

```
select
CM.CUSTNMBR Customer_ID, CM.CUSTNAME Customer_Name,
CM.PYMTRMID Customer_Terms, CM.CUSTCLAS Customer_Class,
CM.PRCLEVEL Price_Level,
```

New terms and **important words** are shown in bold. Words that you see on the screen, for example, in menus or dialog boxes, appear in the text like this: "Clicking the **Next** button moves you to the next screen."

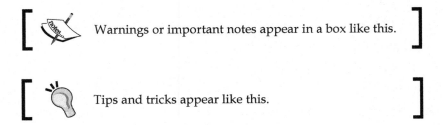

Warnings or important notes appear in a box like this.

Tips and tricks appear like this.

Reader feedback

Feedback from our readers is always welcome. Let us know what you think about this book—what you liked or disliked. Reader feedback is important for us as it helps us develop titles that you will really get the most out of.

To send us general feedback, simply e-mail feedback@packtpub.com, and mention the book's title in the subject of your message.

If there is a topic that you have expertise in and you are interested in either writing or contributing to a book, see our author guide at www.packtpub.com/authors.

Customer support

Now that you are the proud owner of a Packt book, we have a number of things to help you to get the most from your purchase.

Downloading the example code

You can download the example code files from your account at http://www.packtpub.com for all the Packt Publishing books you have purchased. If you purchased this book elsewhere, you can visit http://www.packtpub.com/support and register to have the files e-mailed directly to you.

Downloading the color images of this book

We also provide you with a PDF file that has color images of the screenshots/ diagrams used in this book. The color images will help you better understand the changes in the output. You can download this file from `https://www.packtpub. com/sites/default/files/downloads/9101EN_ColorImages.pdf`.

Errata

Although we have taken every care to ensure the accuracy of our content, mistakes do happen. If you find a mistake in one of our books—maybe a mistake in the text or the code—we would be grateful if you could report this to us. By doing so, you can save other readers from frustration and help us improve subsequent versions of this book. If you find any errata, please report them by visiting `http://www.packtpub. com/submit-errata`, selecting your book, clicking on the **Errata Submission Form** link, and entering the details of your errata. Once your errata are verified, your submission will be accepted and the errata will be uploaded to our website or added to any list of existing errata under the Errata section of that title.

To view the previously submitted errata, go to `https://www.packtpub.com/books/ content/support` and enter the name of the book in the search field. The required information will appear under the **Errata** section.

Piracy

Piracy of copyrighted material on the Internet is an ongoing problem across all media. At Packt, we take the protection of our copyright and licenses very seriously. If you come across any illegal copies of our works in any form on the Internet, please provide us with the location address or website name immediately so that we can pursue a remedy.

Please contact us at `copyright@packtpub.com` with a link to the suspected pirated material.

We appreciate your help in protecting our authors and our ability to bring you valuable content.

Questions

If you have a problem with any aspect of this book, you can contact us at `questions@packtpub.com`, and we will do our best to address the problem.

1
Getting Dynamics CRM 2015 Data into Power BI

Microsoft Dynamics CRM 2015 is a powerful sales automation and relationship management tool with fantastic built-in reporting features. However, when it comes to analyzing data, there is now a more powerful option available with Microsoft Power BI. In this book, we will explore the functionality of using Microsoft Power BI integrated with Microsoft Dynamics CRM 2015. We will show you how to build an interactive sales dashboard, which can be used by everyone (from a salesperson to the CEO).

We will build an interactive sales productivity dashboard that will answer the common salesperson's question: "How is my team doing?" We will build this dashboard with native Microsoft Power BI functionality, including charts, graphs, maps, summaries, and tiles that will be viewable in Microsoft Dynamics CRM 2015 and mobile apps.

This chapter will take you through the following topics:

- How to set up and configure Microsoft Power BI for Office 365
- Connect and access Microsoft Dynamics CRM 2015 datasets
- Explore methods to connect to Dynamics CRM data with Power BI

Preparation

To build the sales productivity dashboard, we must first have the data and tool sets in place in Microsoft Dynamics CRM 2015 and Microsoft Power BI.

Toward the end of this chapter, you should be able to set up and use the following environments to get data for your sales productivity dashboard:

- Microsoft Office 365
- Microsoft Dynamics CRM 2015 Online
- Microsoft Power BI for Office 365

After we connect Power BI with Microsoft Dynamics CRM, we will look at the options to load and query the Dynamics CRM sales data using the Power BI Designer.

Setting up Office 365

Before we start building dashboards with Microsoft Power BI, we have a little setup work to do in Microsoft Office 365, Microsoft Power BI sites, and Microsoft Dynamics CRM Online. The good thing is they live inside the Microsoft Office 365 platform. To use these applications, we first need to set up a Microsoft Office 365 instance and user account. Once we establish the Microsoft Office 365 instance, we can access application subscriptions and manage users who use the Microsoft Office 365 **Admin Portal**.

Here is how it it's done:

1. Navigate to Microsoft Office 365 website using the following link:

   `http://products.office.com/en-us/business/explore-office-365-for-business`

2. Go to **Plans and Pricing** and select the plan type that fits your business. There are a few different plans that can be used with Dynamics CRM Online and Power BI, but in this book, we will use the **Office 365 Enterprise E3** 30-day free trial.

3. Once in the Microsoft Office 365 account setup window, enter your company information and create an account. The account provision process will kick off, and you will be logged in to your Microsoft Office 365 **Admin Portal** shortly after it is provisioned:

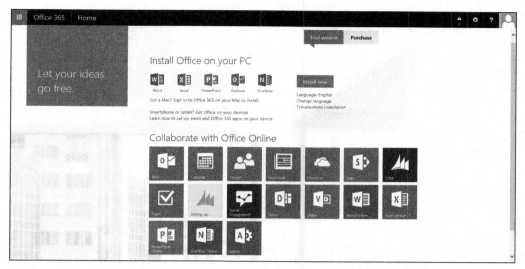

The interface as seen after signing in

Adding Dynamics CRM 2015 Online

Now that we have an active Microsoft Office 365 account, we need to add a Dynamics CRM Online subscription.

 Dynamics CRM On-Premise deployments will integrate with Power BI using an **Internet-facing deployment** (**IFD**) configuration, but in this book, we will use the online version of Dynamics CRM.

To add Dynamics CRM Online to the Office 365 instance, perform the following steps:

1. Navigate to **Purchase Services** in **Admin Portal** and locate the Microsoft Dynamics CRM subscription offering.

2. In this book, we will use the **Microsoft Dynamics CRM Online Professional** 30-day trial.

Giving user access

Before users can connect to a Dynamics CRM Online instance, a license needs to be assigned to a user account. After you assign this license to the user account, you must also assign a security role so that the user can access your Dynamics CRM Organization. Here is how it's done:

1. From the Office 365 **Admin Portal**, select the Dynamics CRM pane from the list of apps:

2. Once in Dynamics CRM, select **Setting | Security | Users** and then navigate to **Users**, who need a role assigned:

    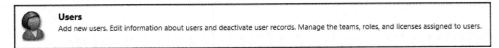

    Users
    Add new users. Edit information about users and deactivate user records. Manage the teams, roles, and licenses assigned to users.

3. Navigate to the user submenu and select **MANAGE ROLES**:

Once the user role is assigned, you should now see the data in Dynamics CRM:

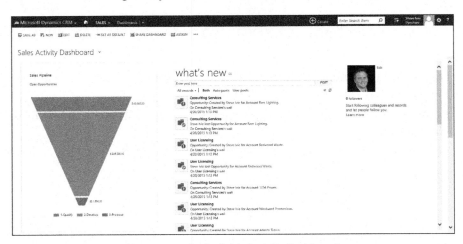

Data as seen in the Sales Activity Dashboard

Importing the sample data

In this book, we will build datasets for a sales productivity dashboard using data from Dynamics CRM the Lead, Account, Opportunity entities. To add the sample data, download the `.csv` files and import them into Dynamics CRM Online with the native import tool.

Here is how you import the sample data:

1. Download the sample `.csv` file from `ContactLead.csv`, `Accounts.csv`, and `Opportunities.csv`.

> You can download the sample files from your account at `http://www.packtpub.com` for all the Packt Publishing books you have purchased. If you purchased this book elsewhere, you can visit `http://www.packtpub.com/support` and register to have the files e-mailed directly to you.

2. In Dynamics CRM, open the import tool located under any list view:

3. Upload the sample `.csv` files and begin the import:

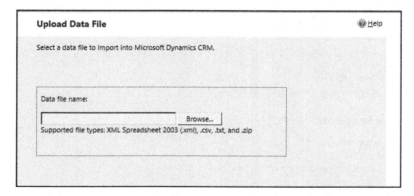

4. Verify mapping and initiate the import data.

Finding the OData connection

Dynamics CRM is a web-based application built on a set of web services. For this book, we will focus on the **Organizational Data Service**, using the **Protocol OData (REST) protocol** to connect Power BI to Dynamics CRM.

Here is how we locate the OData URL in Dynamics CRM to use with Power BI later:

1. In Dynamics CRM, select **Setting | Customizations** in the top navigation bar to access the **Customizations** area.

2. Once in the **Customizations** area, select **Developer Resources** and navigate to **Organizational Data Service** located at the bottom of the browser window:

 Developer Resources
View information or download files that help you develop applications and extensions for Microsoft Dynamics CRM.

3. In **Developer Resources**, scroll down to the bottom of the window and copy the **OData (REST)** URL link. This URL will be used later when you configure the Power BI connection:

Setting up Power BI for the Office 365 site

The *new* Power BI for Office 365 now includes a secure website portal used to store dashboards, reports, and datasets. In *Chapter 7, Deploy and Present Reports to the Power BI Site*, we will show you the features and functionalities of this portal and how to configure and share the site with other users that are both internal and external, but before we do this, we need to set up and configure a new Power BI site.

Here is how it is done:

1. Navigate to Microsoft Power BI for the Office 365 website using the following link:

   ```
   http://www.powerbi.com
   ```

2. Once in the website, enter the e-mail address that was used when you set up the Office 365 account and then submit a request to Power BI for the Office 365 free trial. Shortly after requesting the trial, you will receive an e-mail with a link to access your Power BI site.

3. Once you receive the e-mail, click on the link to the Power BI site and sign in with your specifically created Office 365 user e-mail account.

Sales Productivity Dashboard as seen in Power BI

Installing the Power BI Designer

Power BI along with PowerQuery, PowerMap, and PowerView—used to be only included as a Microsoft Excel 2013 add-in. Although these add-ins are still available, there is now a *new* tool dedicated to Power BI report and dashboard authoring called **Power BI Designer**.

The Power BI Designer offers a lot of the same functionalities as its predecessor in Excel add-in, but without the Excel requirements. The benefit of using the Power BI Designer is that it is a standalone program that can provide self-service data connectivity, transformation, modeling, visualizations, and collaboration. The Power BI Designer is a standalone 64-bit application that can be deployed together with a 32-bit version of Office, using the same functionality that was used to create interactive charts, maps, graphs, and data transformations without the requirement of Microsoft Excel 2013.

Here is how you install it:

1. In the Power BI site, navigate to the down arrow icon located in the top-right corner of the navigation area:

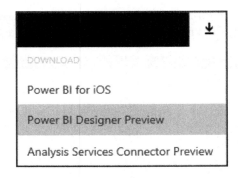

2. Download **Power BI Designer Preview**.

3. Then, install the `PBIDesignr_x64.msi` file.

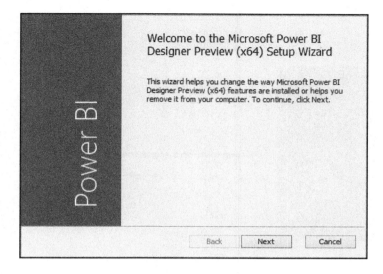

4. Open **Power BI Designer** from the desktop icon:

Now that you have **Power BI Designer** installed and open, you can begin leveraging the tool for dashboard, report creation, and data transformation. Power BI Designer help videos are available at startup or by navigating to **File -> Getting Started** in the main menu.

The Power BI Designer toolset is based on two views:

- **Query**: This connects, shapes, and combines data to data models

- **Report**: This builds reports from the queried information to shareable reports

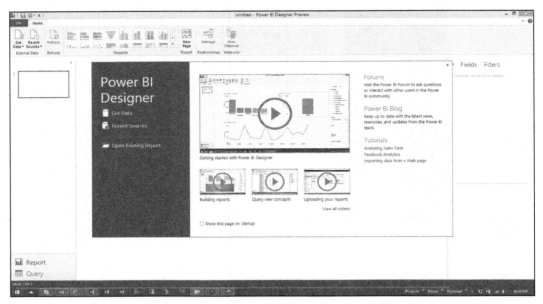

Power BI Designer preview

Once you build your dashboards and reports with **Power BI Designer**, you will want to save your work. Using **Power BI Designer**, you can now save it as a Power BI Designer file. Later in *Chapter 7, Deploy and Present Reports to the Power BI Site*, you will learn how to save the designer file and upload it to the Power BI site.

Reviewing authentication methods

Now that the Power BI Designer is installed, we are ready to connect to the Dynamics CRM data and start building our sales productivity dashboards and reports, but before we do this, we need to understand the various OData (REST) authentication methods provided by Power BI.

Each method is briefly explained here:

- **Anonymous**: This authentication allows any user to access any public content without providing a username and password challenge to the client browser.

- **Windows**: This authentication occurs when your user runs on a corporate network that uses Microsoft Active Directory service domain identities or other Windows accounts to identify users.

- **Basic**: This access authentication is a method for an HTTP user agent to provide a username and password when making a request.

- **The Web API**: This authentication takes place in the host. For web hosting, the host is IIS, which uses HTTP modules for authentication.

- **The marketplace key**: This authentication is based on the subscription-based account key secured through SSL.

- **The Organizational account**: This authentication is based on the users of Dynamics CRM Online, cloud applications, or users who run modern LOB applications on-premises that may leverage a web service such as Azure behind the scenes.

Connecting to Dynamics CRM

You just learned how to set up and configure Power BI sites and the Power BI Designer. Now you will learn how to connect the Power BI Designer to the Dynamics CRM Online instance and put data entities into Power BI.

For our sales productivity dashboard, we will use the following Dynamics CRM entities:

- Users
- Leads
- Accounts
- Opportunities

Checking requirements

Before we connect to Dynamic CRM with the Power BI Designer, let's quickly review the general requirements:

1. A user must specify a valid OData URL for a Dynamics CRM Online instance. The connector will not work with an on-premise CRM version.

2. Enable the OData endpoint in the site settings with Dynamics CRM. Then, select **Settings | Customizations | Developer Resources**. The OData URL is listed under **Service Endpoints**.

3. The user account that you use to access Dynamics CRM Online must be the same as the one you will use for Power BI.

Accessing data

Earlier, we downloaded and installed the Power BI Designer, which allows read-only access to the Dynamics CRM Online instance in order to make it easy for users to get the sales data they want.

To see how easy it is to access data:

1. Open **Power BI Designer** and select **Query** from the bottom-left corner of the **Power BI Designer** window.

2. In the top-left corner of the **Power BI Designer** window, select **Get Data**.

3. In the **Get Data** Window, select **All | Dynamics CRM Online** to access the **Dynamics CRM Online OData Feed** window:

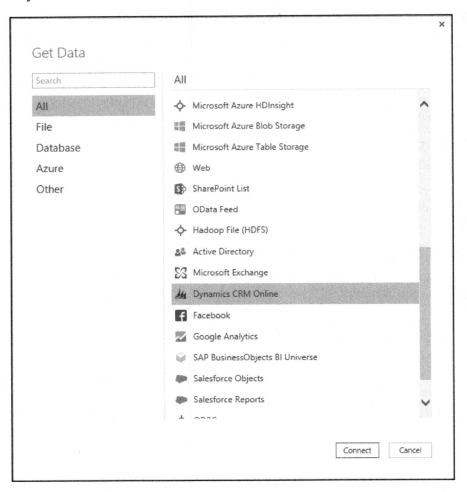

4. Once the **Microsoft Dynamics CRM Online** window opens, enter the Dynamics CRM Online **OData (REST)** URL previously captured during setup:

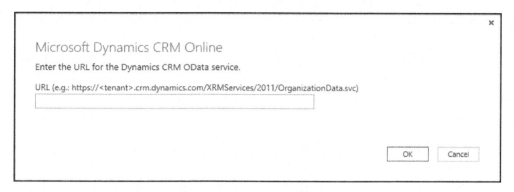

The **Access Dynamics CRM Online OData Feed** window may or may not appear to log in to the Dynamics CRM Online instance. If the window does appear, use **Organizational account** to sign in. For this book, we will select the first URL to connect the OData feed. If the **Access Dynamics CRM Online Odata Feed** window does not appear, you are already connected and authenticated to the Dynamic CRM instance:

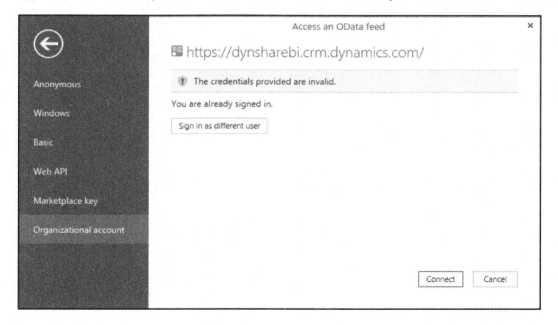

Loading data

Once you have successfully connected to your Dynamics CRM organization, the **Query** functionality of the Power BI Designer runs against the Dynamics CRM Online instance, and the navigator window returns a list of Dynamics CRM data entities to include in your dashboard.

By default, when you load the data to Power BI, all the items will be selected in the navigator window. To individually select multiple items, you will have to check the box to select multiple items.

Here's how you do it:

1. Navigate to the top-left corner of the navigator screen and locate the checkbox labeled **Select Multiple items**.

2. Once this checkbox is ticked, the subarea will include additional checkboxes to individually select the Dynamics CRM data entities.

3. Select the following items from the navigator window:
   ° **AccountSet**
   ° **LeadSet**
   ° **OpportunitySet**
   ° **SystemUserSet**

4. The right-hand side of the navigator window will show you a preview of the fields included and data currently in the dataset.

5. Select **Show Selected** to see a queried list of just the dataset selected:

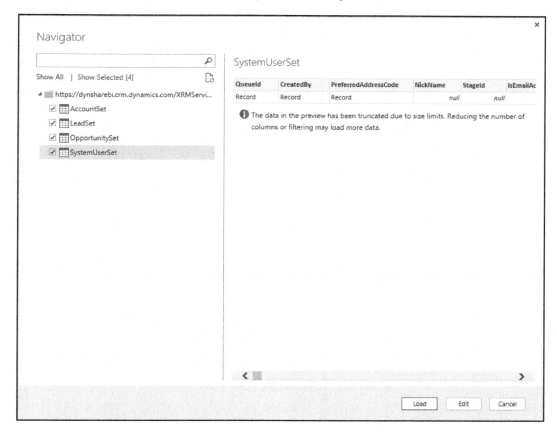

Querying the data

Our next step is to query the Dynamics CRM data that we will load to Power BI. We can do this by editing the query before we load the data or come back later and update the query. By querying only the data we need from Dynamics CRM before loading to Power BI, we can enhance the performance of our reports and dashboards.

Here is how it is done:

1. Select **Edit Query** from the bottom-right hand side of the window; a view of the entity data is presented in **Query view**:

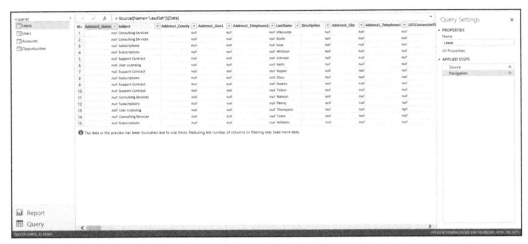

A view of the entity data

2. To modify the query after you load the data, in the top ribbon select **View | Show | Query Settings** to access the **Query Settings** pane.

3. Select **Source** in the **Query Settings** window to update the query entity data:

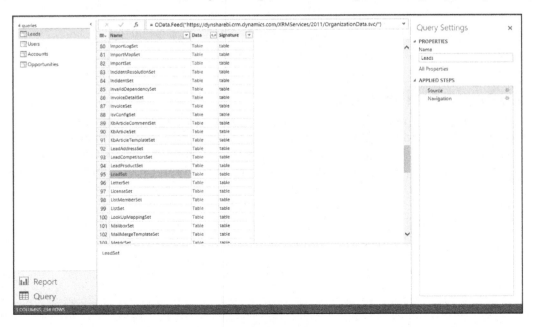

4. In the left-hand side pane, queries are listed and available for selection, viewing, and shaping. In the main pane, data from the selected query is displayed and available for shaping.

Summary

In this chapter, we looked at how to set up our Office 365, Dynamics CRM, and Power BI environments. We deployed the Power BI Designer and connected Dynamics CRM to Power BI in order to retrieve the sales entity data for our sales productivity dashboard.

In the next chapter, we will begin optimizing and consolidating our Dynamic CRM sale datasets. You will start to put together the data that will go into the sales productivity dashboard.

2
Organizing and Consolidating Dynamics CRM 2015 Datasets

The most important part of designing your sales productivity dashboard is the data you have behind it. Think of your dashboards as a house; if you build your house without a solid foundation, no matter what is added to it, it will always fall apart. Sometimes, it is as simple as that. Your dashboards all start with well-planned out foundation of datasets.

Using the Power BI Designer, we will build and review the Dynamics CRM datasets as we go, always ensuring the accuracy of the data and the relationships. Once the datasets are created, we will be able to start organizing and formatting the data so that your sales team can use it.

For a salesperson or manager trying to make reporting and dashboards look clean, the goal is to transform the unstructured datasets into useful sales queries that can be used with the sales productivity reports and dashboard. To achieve this, we need to understand the actual querying and cleanup process from the Power BI Designer.

In this chapter, you will learn how to:

- Organize data relationships
- Add and remove columns
- Prepare column data types
- Format dates and amounts
- Replace list values
- Combine datasets
- Rename column and table names

Before we begin

Since the Dynamics CRM application is based on the relational database model, we already have connected relationships between the entities built-in for us. To leverage the predefined relationships in the Power BI Designer, we need to verify that the setting for **Relationships** is set to detect automatically. Navigate to **File | Options and Settings | Options** and make sure that under **CURRENT FILE**, the **Autodetect new relationships after data is loaded** option is selected:

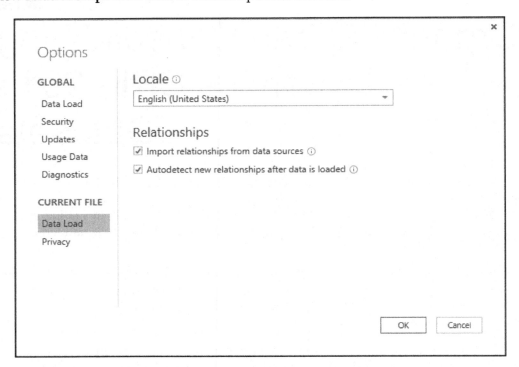

Planning dataset relationships

Now that you have the Power BI Designer setting configured to autodetect the entity relationship, you need to organize the datasets needed for the sales productivity dashboard. To verify this, you will need to review the loaded Dynamic CRM entities and organize the relationships. In this chapter, we will use the following dataset list as the backbone for our sales productivity reports and columns to build the sales productivity dashboard:

- **SystemUserSet** (The Dynamics CRM User table)
    - ○ SystemUserId

- ○ Territory
- ○ Business Unit

- **LeadSet** (Lead Records)
  - ○ LeadId
  - ○ Lead Source

- **OpportunitySet** (Opportunity Records)
  - ○ OpportunityID
  - ○ Originating Lead (LeadSet: LeadId)
  - ○ Account
  - ○ Owner (SystemUserSet: SystemUserId)
  - ○ Estimated Close Date
  - ○ Estimated Amount
  - ○ Actual Close Date
  - ○ Actual Close Amount
  - ○ Sales Stage
  - ○ Status
  - ○ Territory (SystemUserSet: Territory)
  - ○ Business Unit (SystemUserSet: Business Unit)

- **AccountSet** (Account Records)
  - ○ AccountId
  - ○ AccountNumber
  - ○ Address1_City
  - ○ Address1_StateOrProvince

Understanding the querying process

When you organize your Dynamics CRM datasets in the Power BI Designer, you can use the query view; you are basically running a SQL SELECT query against the Dynamics CRM data. At no time is the underlying Dynamics CRM data ever affected by the query. Only views of the data are adjusted and shaped.

Here are a few examples of the steps included in a query:

- Renaming a table
- Changing a data type
- Deleting columns
- Joining to tables

Every time a Power BI query connects to the Dynamics CRM (OData) data source, each individual step is processed so that the data is always rendered the way you specified. This process occurs whenever you use the query. It could be in the Power BI Designer or shared as a Power BI Service.

Each step is captured sequentially in **Query Settings | APPLIED STEPS**:

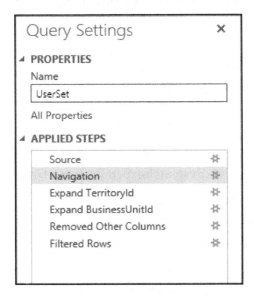

Removing unused columns

Looking at every field in a dataset can become cumbersome and confusing, so the first thing you want to do to organize these Dynamic CRM datasets is to remove unused columns. This will help the performance as well as the view ability of each datasets. Using the dataset list, you need to design a query that only uses the columns that will be used in the reports in the sales productivity dashboard.

The home ribbon on the main Power BI Query window gives you a lot of different options to add and remove columns and records from a dataset. For this book, we will focus on choosing just the columns we need for each dataset.

If at any time you did need to add or remove just one column at a time, this option is available in the home ribbon or by right-clicking on a column and choosing from the menu that appears.

Here is an example of how to do it:

1. Using the **System User** dataset, first remove columns by navigating to the home ribbon tab in the Power BI Designer and select **Choose Columns** under the **Manage Columns** section:

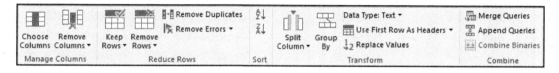

2. Check the **TerritoryId**, **BusinessUnitId**, and **SystemUserId** fields in the **Choose Columns** selection window:

3. Now, click on **OK**; you will only see the columns you selected in the query window:

	TerritoryId.Name	BusinessUnitId.Name	SystemUserId
1	Northest	Dynamics AX	88dc6ce9-9fbb-e411-80ea-c4346bac094c
2	Midwest	Dynamics AX	42a01163-a0bb-e411-80ea-c4346bac094c
3	Southeast	Dynamics CRM	bbd99d15-a0bb-e411-80e8-c4346bac3acc
4	Midwest	Dynamics GP	ee19e680-a0bb-e411-80e8-c4346bac3acc
5	Northest	Dynamics AX	f819e680-a0bb-e411-80e8-c4346bac3acc
6	Northest	Dynamics GP	64b28425-a0bb-e411-80ea-c4346bad3674
7	Southeast	Office 365	08c9ce90-a0bb-e411-80ea-c4346bad3674
8	Southeast	Dynamics GP	de3aafa2-a0bb-e411-80ea-c4346bad3674
9	West Coast	Dynamics AX	001773c6-a0bb-e411-80ea-c4346bad3674
10	Northest	Dynamics CRM	d9ffe6cd-a5bb-e411-80ea-c4346bad3674

4. From the **Choose Columns** selection window for the **LeadSet** dataset, select **LeadSourceCode.Value** and **LeadId** fields and then click on **OK**. Now, you will only see the columns you selected in the query window:

	LeadSourceCode.Value	LeadId
1	Trade Show	07df8303-19e7-e411-80f4-c4346bac3acc
2	Web	09df8303-19e7-e411-80f4-c4346bac3acc
3	Web	0bdf8303-19e7-e411-80f4-c4346bac3acc
4	Advertisement	0ddf8303-19e7-e411-80f4-c4346bac3acc
5	Employee Referral	0fdf8303-19e7-e411-80f4-c4346bac3acc
6	Web	11df8303-19e7-e411-80f4-c4346bac3acc
7	Trade Show	13df8303-19e7-e411-80f4-c4346bac3acc
8	Web	15df8303-19e7-e411-80f4-c4346bac3acc
9	Employee Referral	17df8303-19e7-e411-80f4-c4346bac3acc
10	Advertisement	19df8303-19e7-e411-80f4-c4346bac3acc
11	Web	1bdf8303-19e7-e411-80f4-c4346bac3acc
12	Trade Show	1ddf8303-19e7-e411-80f4-c4346bac3acc
13	Web	1fdf8303-19e7-e411-80f4-c4346bac3acc
14	Trade Show	21df8303-19e7-e411-80f4-c4346bac3acc

5. From the **Choose Columns** selection window for the **OpportunitySet** dataset, select **ParentAccountId, OwnerId, ActualCloseDate, ActualValue, SalesStage, EstimatedCloseDate, EstimatedValue, OrginatingLeadId, StateCode**, and **OpportunityId**. Then, click on **OK**; you will only see the columns you selected in the query window:

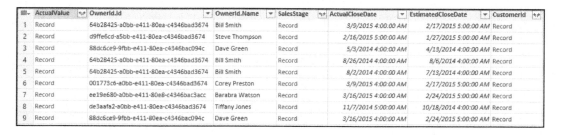

6. From the **Choose Columns** selection window for the **AccountSet** dataset, select the **AccountId, AccountNumber, Address1_City**, and **Address1_StateOrProvince** fields. Click on **OK**; you will only see the columns you selected in the query window:

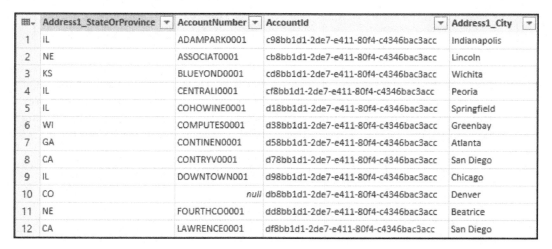

Preparing column data types

Now that you understand the query process and what datasets you need to connect together, let's see how to modify the data. You will need to modify data types in each Dynamic CRM dataset list mentioned before.

We will start with the **OpportunitySet**; here is how we do it:

1. In Power Designer, select the **OpportunitySet** dataset from the left-hand side menu of the Power BI query window:

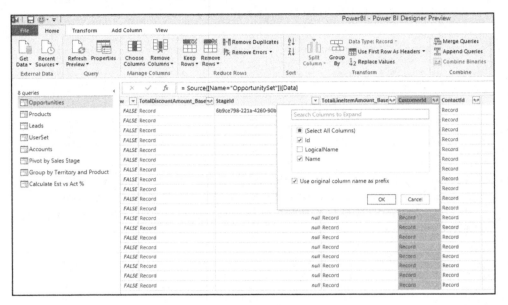

2. Once in the query view of the **OpportunitySet** dataset, select and change the column data type for **CustomerId** to show the name. To do this, click on the icon 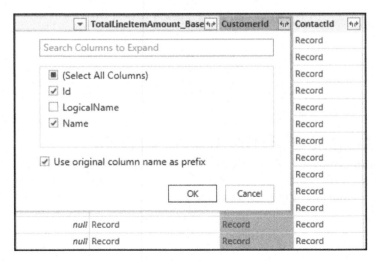 with the **CustomerId** header name and change the column data type to **Id** and **Name**. This will produce two columns for both data types:

Staying in the **OpportunitySet** dataset, click on the icon with the **OrginatingLeadID** header name and change the column data type to **ID**. This will show the Dynamics CRM GUID for each **Lead** record:

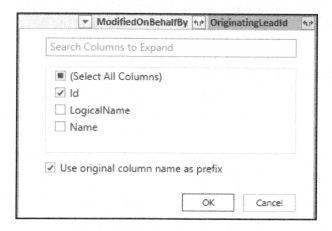

For the **OwnerID**, click on the icon with the **OwnerID** header name and change the column data type to **Id** and **Name**. This will produce two columns for both data types:

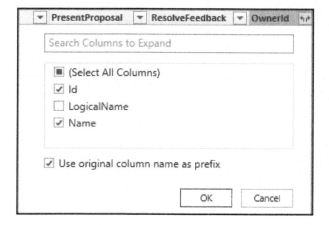

3. Following the same process, select the **SystemUserSet** dataset from the left-hand side of the Power BI query window.

   ○ For **TerritoryID**, click on the icon with the **TerritoryID** header name and change the column data type to **Name**

   ○ For **BusinessUnitID**, click on the icon with the **BusinessUnitID** header name and change the column data type to **Name**

- ° Following the same process, select the **LeadSet** dataset from the left-hand side of the Power BI query window
- ° For the **LeadSourceCode** column, click on the icon with the **LeadSourceCode** header name and reset the column data type to **Value** by unchecking and then rechecking the box

Filtering column values

At times, you may need to filter your data to reduce the number of records loaded in your dataset. The Power BI Designer provides you options to remove rows, duplicates, and errors and filter by individual columns values.

Dynamics CRM is built to store a lot of data, so you need to create filters for the **SystemUserSet** that remove users that are not sales users.

Here is how you perform this for the **SystemUserSet** dataset:

1. In Power BI, select the **SystemUserSet** dataset from the left-hand side of the query window.

2. Select the icon with the **BusinessUnitId** header name, click on the **Text Filters** menu item, and select **Does Not Contain…**:

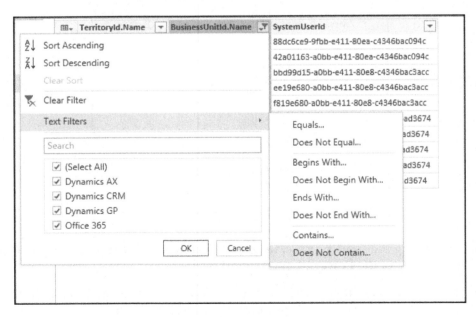

3. Once the **Filter Rows** window appears, select the value you do not want to show in the **SystemUserSet** dataset. For this book, we will select the business unit named **dynsharebi**.

> **Dynsharebi** is the Dynamics CRM Organization name for this instance. For your instance, the name will be different.

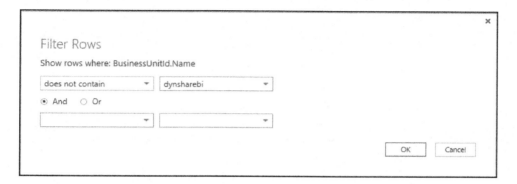

4. Then, click on **OK**. Now, the **SystemUserSet** dataset will not show any records that include **dynsharebi** in the **BusinessUnitId** column:

⊞	TerritoryId.Name	BusinessUnitId.Name	SystemUserId
1	Northest	Dynamics AX	88dc6ce9-9fbb-e411-80ea-c4346bac094c
2	Midwest	Dynamics AX	42a01163-a0bb-e411-80ea-c4346bac094c
3	Southeast	Dynamics CRM	bbd99d15-a0bb-e411-80e8-c4346bac3acc
4	Midwest	Dynamics GP	ee19e680-a0bb-e411-80e8-c4346bac3acc
5	Northest	Dynamics AX	f819e680-a0bb-e411-80e8-c4346bac3acc
6	Northest	Dynamics GP	64b28425-a0bb-e411-80ea-c4346bad3674
7	Southeast	Office 365	08c9ce90-a0bb-e411-80ea-c4346bad3674
8	Southeast	Dynamics GP	de3aafa2-a0bb-e411-80ea-c4346bad3674
9	West Coast	Dynamics AX	001773c6-a0bb-e411-80ea-c4346bad3674
10	Northest	Dynamics CRM	d9ffe6cd-a5bb-e411-80ea-c4346bad3674

Combining datasets

Now that you have the columns updated and filters in place, you need to start connecting the datasets. Although there are many different options to connect these datasets to get the results you need for your dashboard, in this book, we will join **LeadSet**, **SystemUserSet**, **OpportunitySet**, and **AccountSet** together to create our two queries.

Let's start by connecting the **LeadSet** and **SystemUserSet** datasets to **OpportunitySet** to show the lead source, territory, and business unit columns in the **OpportunitySet** dataset. First, we will join the **LeadSet** dataset to the **OpportunitySet** dataset to display the **LeadSourceCode** column.

Here is how you will join the **LeadSourceCode** column:

1. From the **OpportunitySet** query view window, select **Merge Queries** from the home ribbon:

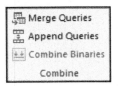

2. Once the **Merge Queries** window appears, select **LeadSet** from the list that appears at the bottom grid:

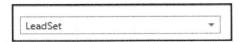

3. Locate and highlight **OrginatingLeadId** from the **OpportunitySet** dataset located at the top grid and join it to **LeadSet LeadID** located at the bottom grid:

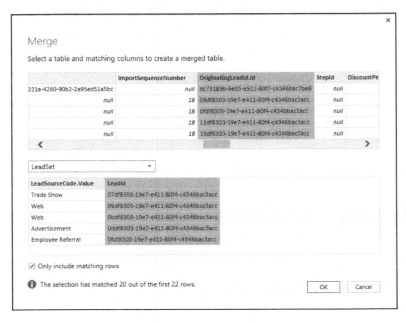

4. Then, click on **OK**. A new column will appear at the end of the **Opportunity** dataset.

5. Now, click on the icon with the **NewColumn** header name and select the **LeadId** and **LeadSourceCode.Value** fields:

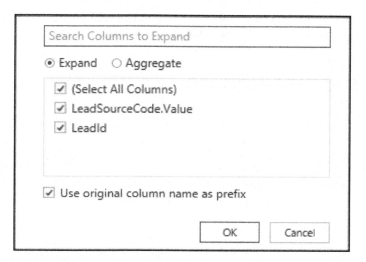

6. The new column will show the **Record** or **Null** entries; to transform these data types, we need to click on the icon with the **NewColumn. LeadSourceCode** header name and recheck **Value**.

7. The **LeadSet** dataset numeric pick list number for **LeadSourceCode** will now show in the column.

> Later in this section, we will translate the numeric pick list value into an actual text field that shows the lead source name.

Now that we have **LeadSourceCode** on the **OpportunitySet** dataset, we will perform the same operation with **SystemUserSet** to get **TerritoryID** and **BusinessUnitID**.

Here is how you add these two columns:

1. From the **OpportunitySet** query view window, select **Merge Queries** from the home ribbon.

2. Once the **Merge Queries** window appears, select **SystemUserSet** from the pick list located at the bottom grid.

3. Locate and highlight **OwnerID** from **OpportunitySet** located at the top grid and join it to **SystemUserSet SystemUserID** located at the bottom grid.

4. Click on **OK**. A new column will appear at the end of the **Opportunity** dataset.

5. Then, select **All Columns** to uncheck all fields.

6. Click on the icon [⁺ⁱ⁺] with the **NewColumn** header name and select the **TerritoryID** and **BusinessUnitID** fields.

7. Now, click on **OK**. A new column for **TerritoryID** and **BusinessUnitID** will appear at the end of the **OpportunitySet** dataset.

Replacing list values

Dynamics CRM stores the pick list values as numbers for fields, such as **Status**, **SalesStage**, and **Lead Source**. Sometimes, you need to change the numeric values to actual text in a column. The Power BI Designer makes it easy for us to do just this by adjusting the data types directly from the home ribbon or column.

The **OpportunitySet** and **LeadSet** datasets require column updates to show the actual pick list names. We will start with **OpportunitySet**.

Here is what we will do:

1. In the Power BI Designer, select the **OpportunitySet** dataset from the left-hand side of the query window.

2. In the **SalesStage** column, click on the icon [▼] with the **SalesStage** header name and reset the column data type to **Value** by unchecking and then rechecking the box.

3. Highlight the **SalesStage.Value** column and change the data type to text in the home ribbon:

▼	SalesStage.Value	▼	
	3		
	3		
	3		
	3		
	3		
	3		
	2		
	3		
	3		
	0		
	3		
	1		

4. Once the column values change to text, select a single value from the column:

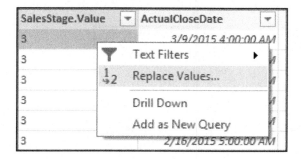

5. Click on the **Replace Values...** link in the home ribbon to access the **Replace Values** form. You can also do this step by right-clicking on a single value and using the quick menu:

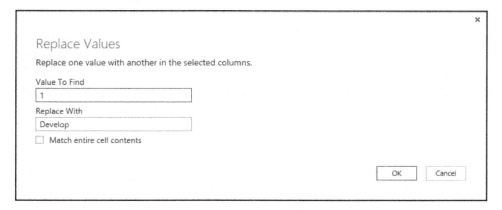

6. Use the following list to translate the pick list values and then repeat the process for each value. To review mappings in Dynamics CRM, verify that you have the system customizer roles and then navigate to **Customizations** and open the entity you are querying from. Select the attribute and review the pick list values:

  - 0 = Qualify
  - 1 = Develop
  - 2 = Propose
  - 3 = Close

7. Once you replace each number with the **SalesStage** name and click on **OK**, you will see the values updated to text fields in the query view window:

8. To adjust the **StateCode** column, click on the icon  with the **StateCode** header name and reset the column data type to **Value** by unchecking and then rechecking the box.

9. Follow the same preceding process along with the following list to translate the pick list values for **StateCode** and then repeat the process for each value:

     ° 0 = Open

     ° 1 = Won

     ° 2 = Lost

10. Follow the same process for the **LeadSet** dataset. In Power BI, select the **LeadSet** dataset from the left-hand side of the query window. Then, use the following list to translate the pick list values and repeat the process for each value:

     ° 1 = Advertisement

     ° 2 = Employee Referral

     ° 3 = External Referral

     ° 4 = Partner

     ° 5 = Public Relations

     ° 6 = Seminar

     ° 7 = Trade Show

     ° 8 = Web

     ° 9 = Word of Mouth

     ° 10 = Other

Formatting amounts and dates

The good thing about the Dynamics CRM is that it already has the correct formats you need for amounts and dates because of the data structure of this application. In *Chapter 3, Building Summaries and Custom Calculations,* you will be able to build sales summaries with the newly created datasets by pivoting and grouping the data. There may be a case where we need to format the dates or amounts while doing this.

Here is an example of how to format amounts:

1. In Power BI, select the **OpportunitySet** dataset from the left-hand side of the query window [▼].

2. For the **EstimatedAmount** or **ActualAmount** column, click on the icon with the **EstimatedAmount** or **ActualAmount** header name and reset the column data type to *value* by unchecking and then rechecking the box.

3. Highlight the **EstimatedAmount** or **ActualAmount** column and change the **Data Type** to **Decimal Number** in the home ribbon:

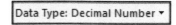

4. Once the column values are changed to decimal, the column data types will be updated to decimal amounts:

⊞▾	Amount ▼	Estimated Amount ▼
1	94800.82	95000
2	22469.39	22000
3	300	300
4	34000	34000
5	19000	15000
6	150000	150000
7	null	10800
8	34000	30000

Here is an example of how to format dates:

1. In Power BI, select the **OpportunitySet** dataset from the left-hand side of the query window.

2. For the **EstimatedCloseDate** or **ActualCloseDate** column, click on the icon [▼] with the **EstimatedCloseDate** or **ActualCloseDate** header name and reset the column data type to **Value** by unchecking and then rechecking the box.

3. Highlight the **EstimatedCloseDate** or **ActualCloseDate** column and change the **Data Type** to **Date/Time** in the home ribbon:

Data Type: Date/Time ▾

4. Once the column values are changed to **Date/Time**, the column data types will be updated to show the dates:

Close Date	Estimated Close Date
3/9/2015 4:00:00 AM	2/17/2015 5:00:00 AM
2/16/2015 5:00:00 AM	1/27/2015 5:00:00 AM
null	4/20/2015 4:00:00 AM
5/3/2014 4:00:00 AM	4/13/2014 4:00:00 AM
8/26/2014 4:00:00 AM	8/6/2014 4:00:00 AM
null	12/10/2014 5:00:00 AM
8/2/2014 4:00:00 AM	7/13/2014 4:00:00 AM
3/9/2015 4:00:00 AM	2/17/2015 5:00:00 AM

Renaming datasets and columns

From time to time, you may need to rename a dataset or individual column header title to make it easier later to build your reports and dashboards. For the sales productivity reports and dashboard, let's rename the dataset and update a few column header titles in the **OpportunitySet** dataset.

Here is how you rename a dataset:

1. Select the **OpportunitySet** dataset from the left-hand side of the Power BI query window.

2. Right-click and select **Properties** from the quick menu.

3. Replace **OpportunitySet** to **Opportunities**:

4. Repeat the steps for the other datasets using the following list:
   - SystemUserSet = **Users**
   - LeadSet = **Leads**
   - AccountSet = **Accounts**

5. After updating the dataset names, you should see the following in the left-hand side of the query menu:

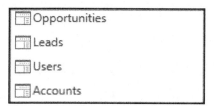

Now, let's rename a few column titles. There are a couple of ways to rename a column. You can select the column and then rename it from the main ribbon or just right-click on the column and select **Rename** from the quick menu.

Finally, let's update the column titles in the **OpportunitySet** dataset so that our reports look better later.

Here is how you rename a column:

1. Select the **Opportunities** dataset from the left-hand side of the Power BI query window.

2. Highlight a column title header. Then, right-click and select **Rename** from the quick menu or select the **Rename** link under the **Transform** ribbon.

3. Once the cursor appears on the column title header, update the column title name.

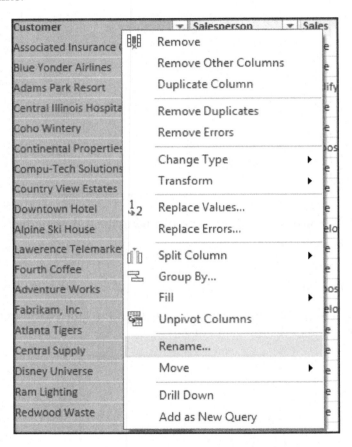

Although you can use any titles you want, for this book we will use the following list for the column header titles:

Opportunities

- ActualValue = Amount
- ActualCloseDate = Close Date
- EstimatedValue = Estimated Amount
- EstimatedCloseDate = Estimated Close Date
- OwnerId.Name = Salesperson
- SaleStage.Value = Sales Stage
- CustomerID.Name = Customer
- StateCode.Value = Status
- NewColumn.TerriotyId.Name = Territory
- NewColumn.BusinessUnitId.Name = Practice

Summary

In this chapter, we looked at how to transform our Dynamics CRM data into two main queried datasets for opportunities and products. We shaped our data using the built-in functionality of the Power BI Designer to modify and then filter columns, data types, and list values.

In the next chapter, we will use our newly transformed datasets to create rollup summaries and then start laying out the dashboard. You will also start putting together the pivot tables and grouping for your summary level details that will go into the sales productivity dashboard.

3
Building Summaries and Custom Calculations

Every salesperson has a different way to look at their data. Some may like it at a high-level territory or practice the sales pipeline overview, whereas others may like to see data at a micro level, drilling through to individual salesperson performance. Either way, providing a dashboard with a summary of the data real time is a huge advantage to every user.

Now that we have all our core datasets built-in the Power BI Designer, we can start to construct our summary-level information. An interactive sales dashboard with summary information can be built with a simple grouping or pivoting, just like you would in Excel.

Using the Power BI Designer, let's prepare the data for salespersons to see summary-level totals. To do this, we need to group and pivot the Dynamics CRM sales datasets to show the sales summary information, including sales by status and stage, lost revenue by product and territory, and calculate the number of days a sales opportunity has been open. You will be able to leverage these summary-level information to build truly interactive sales productivity reports and dashboards.

In this chapter, you will learn how to:

- Group rows
- Pivot columns
- Add custom calculations

Creating duplicate datasets

Before you begin to create your summarized datasets, you need to make duplicate copies of the current opportunity and product datasets to work from. In this book, you need to create three new duplicate datasets based on the main opportunities dataset to be used for the sales productivity report summary information. Perform the following steps:

1. Navigate to the **Opportunities** dataset, right-click on it, and select **Duplicate**:

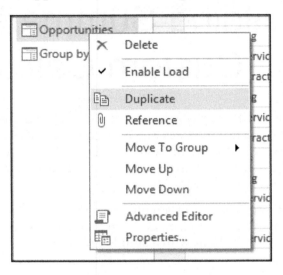

2. Once the duplicate table is created, follow the same methods you learned in *Chapter 2, Organizing and Consolidating Dynamics CRM 2015 Datasets* for renaming a dataset and removing columns. Use the following list as guidance:

   ° Group by territory and product:

   Territory

   Name

   Amount

   ° Pivot by sales stage:

   Practice

   Salesperson

   Qualify

   Develop

   Propose

> ° Calculated days for open sales:
>
>> Name
>>
>> Customer
>>
>> Practice
>>
>> Estimated Amount
>>
>> Days Open

Grouping rows

Most of the time, users want to see their summary sales data in individual sales revenue buckets that follow some sort of sales process. An example of this would be to group the sum of multiple rows into one row based on territory and product. The Power BI Designer gives us the tools to do just that.

Here is how it is done:

From the main ribbon on the main Power BI query window, you can group any combination of rows in a dataset. For this book, we will focus on a combination of groupings for territory and product to get summarized data for the sales productivity reports and dashboards.

Here is what we need to do to group a dataset:

1. First, we will address **Group by Territory and Product**. In the **Group by Territory and Product** dataset, navigate to the home ribbon tab in the Power BI Designer and select **Group By** under the **Transform** tab:

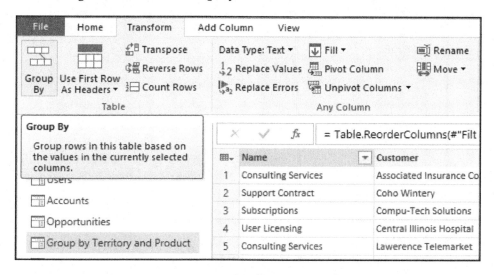

2. Once the **Group By** window appears, use the **+** or **-** sign to add the columns you want to group by. Use the **Name**, **Territory**, and **Status** columns for this summary dataset.

3. Now, add the aggregate **New column name**, **Operation**, and **Column** for the outputted row count and the total sum amount information:

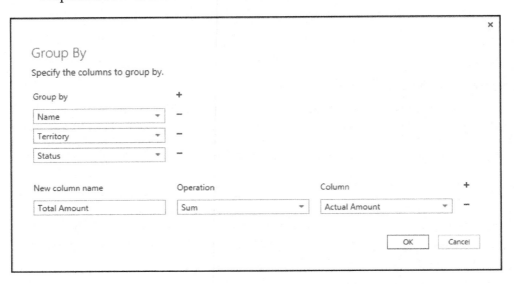

4. After you click on **OK**, the query executes the **Group By** operation and returns aggregated summary results:

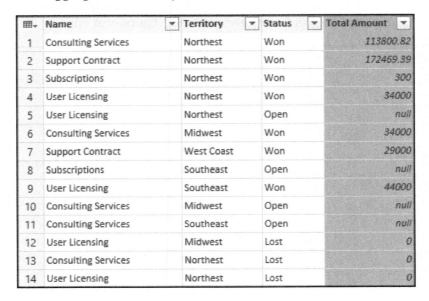

⊞▾	Name	Territory	Status	Total Amount
1	Consulting Services	Northest	Won	113800.82
2	Support Contract	Northest	Won	172469.39
3	Subscriptions	Northest	Won	300
4	User Licensing	Northest	Won	34000
5	User Licensing	Northest	Open	null
6	Consulting Services	Midwest	Won	34000
7	Support Contract	West Coast	Won	29000
8	Subscriptions	Southeast	Open	null
9	User Licensing	Southeast	Won	44000
10	Consulting Services	Midwest	Open	null
11	Consulting Services	Southeast	Open	null
12	User Licensing	Midwest	Lost	0
13	Consulting Services	Northest	Lost	0
14	User Licensing	Northest	Lost	0

If at any time you need to reverse the grouping, you can use the cancel icon ☒ to cancel the step from the Query Settings window located on the right-hand side of the Power BI Designer query form.

Pivot columns

At another time, you may need to pivot columns so that you can aggregate values for each unique value in a column. For example, if you need to know how many opportunities are there in each stage and what the total amount is for each stage, you may use a pivot table. Just like Excel, the Power BI Designer works the same way.

To build a good example for this, use the **Pivot by Sales Stage** dataset we created earlier. The new dataset needs to eventually show the count of opportunities and total amounts by **Sales Stage**.

This is how you do it:

1. Open the **Pivot by Sales Stage** dataset in the query window and select the column that you want to pivot from. In our case, this will be the **Sales Stage** column.

2. After you have the column selected, navigate to the **Transform | Pivot Column** tab from the main ribbon to open the pivot window:

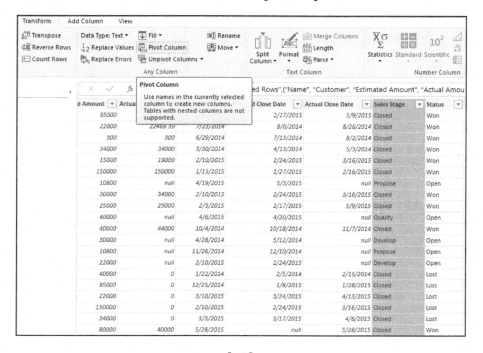

3. Once the **Pivot Column** window appears, it will show you the column that you will use to pivot the data on. Select **Estimated Amount** from the **Values Column** pick list. We will use the default value under **Advanced options** in this book, but if you do need to use it in the future, it may be used to select the functions that will be applied to the aggregated values:

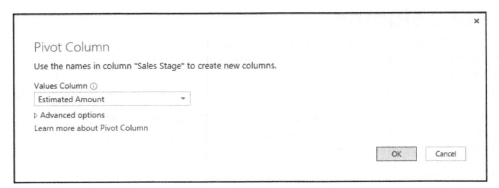

4. After you click on **OK**, the query window will display the summary data based on the pivoted configuration:

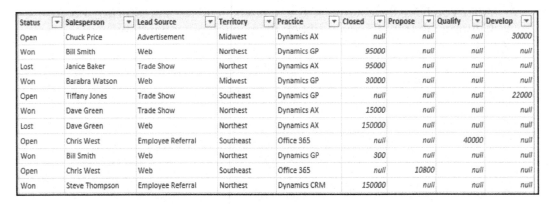

Status	Salesperson	Lead Source	Territory	Practice	Closed	Propose	Qualify	Develop
Open	Chuck Price	Advertisement	Midwest	Dynamics AX	null	null	null	30000
Won	Bill Smith	Web	Northest	Dynamics GP	95000	null	null	null
Lost	Janice Baker	Trade Show	Northest	Dynamics AX	95000	null	null	null
Won	Barabra Watson	Web	Midwest	Dynamics GP	30000	null	null	null
Open	Tiffany Jones	Trade Show	Southeast	Dynamics GP	null	null	null	22000
Won	Dave Green	Trade Show	Northest	Dynamics AX	15000	null	null	null
Lost	Dave Green	Web	Northest	Dynamics AX	150000	null	null	null
Open	Chris West	Employee Referral	Southeast	Office 365	null	null	40000	null
Won	Bill Smith	Web	Northest	Dynamics GP	300	null	null	null
Open	Chris West	Web	Southeast	Office 365	null	10800	null	null
Won	Steve Thompson	Employee Referral	Northest	Dynamics CRM	150000	null	null	null

Calculating fields

The Power BI Designer gives you the options to add the custom date, time, and duration formulas to your datasets with simple menu selections. These formulas operate in the same way an Excel formula would if you were using the Power BI add-in for Excel. In this example, we will create a simple formula to calculate the number of days an opportunity has been open using the built-in functionality from the Power BI Designer.

Here is how we do this using the **Opportunities** dataset:

1. In the query view window, highlight the **Created On** column and then select **Date | Age** from the main menu bar under **Add Column**:

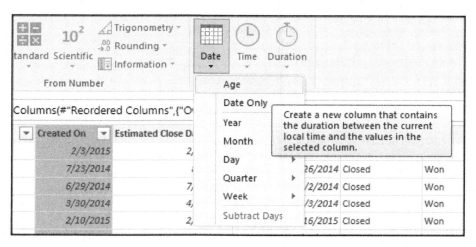

2. A new column called **AgeFromDate** will be created at the end of the dataset with the total number of days down to the second. Once the column appears, select **Duration | Total Days** from the main menu bar under **Add Column** to change the values to just the number for days:

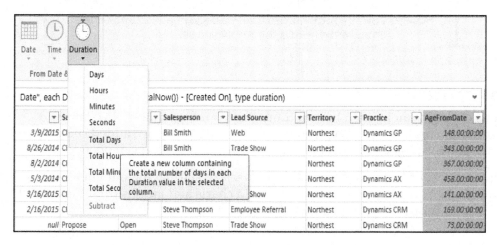

3. Rename the column to **Days Open** to prepare the dataset for the reports.

4. For advanced calculations, you can adjust the actual formulas with **Advanced Editor** or **Formula Bar** from the main menu bar under **View**.

The formulas for power query syntax are listed at `https://support.office.com/en-us/article/Power-Query-formula-categories-125024ec-873c-47b9-bdfd-b437f8716819`.

Summary

In this chapter, you learned how to transform your Dynamics CRM data into three summary datasets with grouping and pivoting. We also added some custom calculation to show the number of days an opportunity has been open.

In the next chapter, you will use all the datasets to start laying out your reports and dashboards. You will also learn how to build charts and graphs from the datasets and how to frame the sales productivity dashboard.

4
Improving the Look and Feel by Adding Charts, Tables, and Maps

The goal to build the sales productivity dashboard is to graphically present the Dynamics CRM data for sales pipeline and revenue reporting to help make the information simpler and easy to understand.

Improving the look and feel of the reports that will be included in the sales productivity dashboard will help simplify the datasets we created in *Chapter 3, Building Summaries and Custom Calculations*. Adding different visualizations to the reports using the Power BI Designer, including charts and maps, can reveal a lot about the data. We will not cover every option, just the most common charts used for sales reporting.

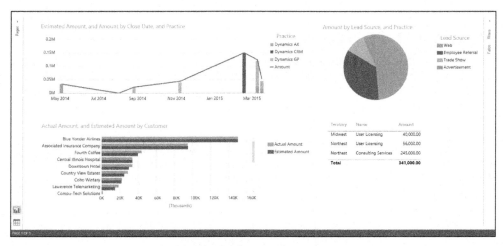

Sales Productivity Report

In this chapter, you will learn how to add graphical representations to the sales productivity report pages. This will include seven different data visualization options, including the following:

- The deals closed stacked combo chart
- The closed won by lead source pie chart
- The lost deals by territory table
- The top accounts closed-clustered column chart
- The practice revenue by sales stage-stacked bar chart
- The revenue by state and practice-filled map
- The deals open days card

Getting visual

There are many different options available to visualize data using Power BI. In this chapter, we will use a few different examples, and each example is meant to be a baseline to understand how the Power BI reports work with charts, maps, and tables.

Later in *Chapter 6, Adding ERP Data*, we will pin down individual visualization from each report to our sales productivity dashboard. One thing to note here is that not all the report visualization options can be pinned at this time. As Power BI continues to evolve, there will be more options available.

The most updated pinnable visualizations can be reviewed at https://support. powerbi.com/knowledgebase/articles/611046.

Starting a report

You can build reports using either the Power BI Designer or Power BI for the Office 365 site. In this chapter, we will build the reports with the Power BI Designer and then in *Chapter 6, Adding ERP Data*, we will import and modify the reports using Power BI for Office 365 sites.

 If you have ever used Microsoft Excel with Power View, the Power BI Designer and Power BI for Office 365 work the same way; the reports will be presented in the left-hand side pane and the individual datasets will be presented in the right-hand side pane.

Building a report with the Power BI Designer is fairly simple. Starting with a blank report canvas, we will add all the data visualizations with a drag and drop method from the datasets fields located on the left-hand side of the Power BI Designer window. We will build each visualization on its own report for clarity purposes.

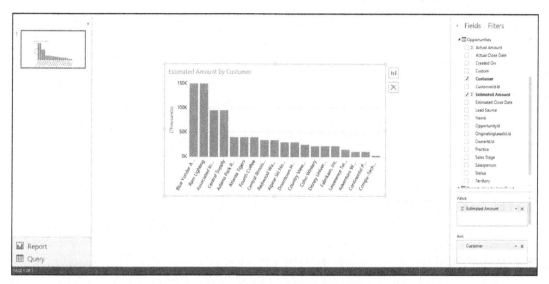

Bar graph Estimated Amount by Customer

Most of these reports will be built using the **Opportunities** dataset, but we will also use the **Grouped** and **Pivoted** datasets to show some different options.

Let's get started:

1. In the Power BI Designer, navigate to the **Report** area in the main form window and start a new report:

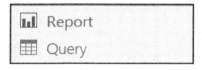

2. Get familiar with the **Report** canvas by navigating to the **Fields** area located on the right-hand side of the Power BI window and verifying that all the queried dataset information is present.

3. There may be symbols for aggregation (∑) and Geo-Map (⊕) for some of the fields in each dataset. By default, Power BI adds these fields based on data types:

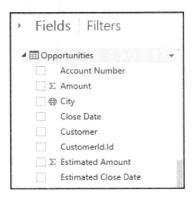

The stacked combo chart

The first report we need to build will be based on the **Opportunities** queried dataset. We need to show all **Deals Closed by Date**. A good chart to use for this is a stacked combo chart that includes the bar and the common line charts.

Using this stacked combo chart, we will be able to gain visual insights into the sales revenue trending over time by **Practice** compared against the overall **Amount**. This report should expose negative and positive selling trends. In the future, it may even be used to predict future sales decisions.

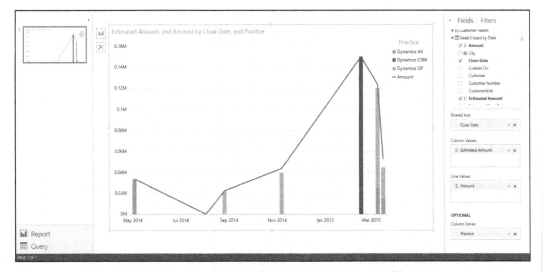

Stacked Combo Chart Estimated Amount by Close Data and Practice

In this line chart, we need to organize the reporting measures based on the **Amount** and **Closed Date** fields.

Let's build the chart. Perform the following steps:

1. Navigate to the **Fields** and **Filters** area on the left-hand side of the form window and select **Practice**, **Amount**, and **Close Date** from the **Opportunities** queried dataset:

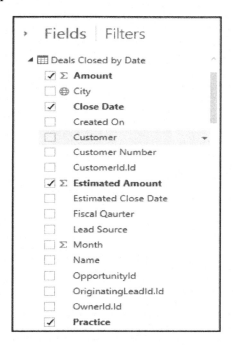

2. The default chart shown will always be a vertical bar chart; to change this to the stacked combo chart, use the floating menu icon located in the left-side corner of the chart or the main menu chart icon located in the selection area:

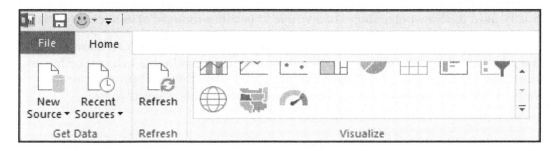

3. To resize the chart, select and drag any side or corner of the chart area.

4. Verify that the **Column Values**, **Line Values**, **Shared Axis**, and **Column Series** fields are correct by navigating to the **Fields** and **Filters** area located on the right-hand side of the Power BI window:

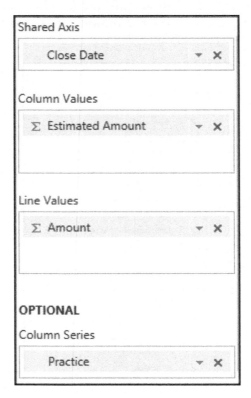

The pie chart

Building the line chart was pretty easy. Now, let's build something a little more interesting. Another common chart used in Power BI is the pie chart. The pie chart is mostly used to show percentages of a whole. It is better thought of as slices of a pizza.

Seeing a visual representation of the sales revenue won from each lead source, such as a telemarketing campaign or an e-mail campaign, is invaluable to a marketing and sales team. The pie chart can be used to quickly identify the best option(s) for the lead generation process based on the most important value: sales revenue.

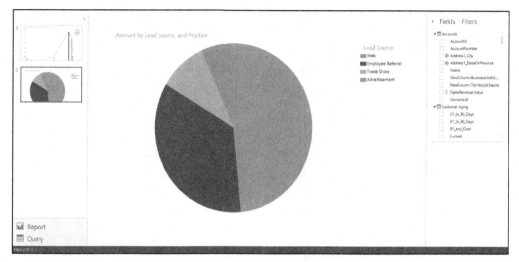

Pie Chart Amounts by Source and Practice

For our sales productivity dashboard, we need to add the new report canvas and the pie chart, which shows **Closed Won by Lead Source**. Again, we will use the queried **Opportunities** dataset fields, but this time, we need to add a chart legend based on **Lead Sources**.

Here is how to build it:

1. To add a new page to your report for the pie chart, navigate to the top main menu and select **New Page**:

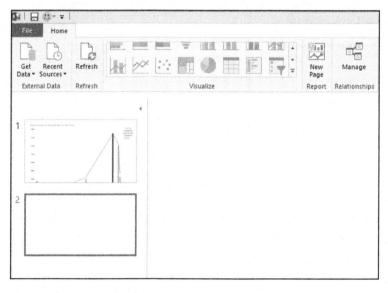

2. Navigate to the **Fields** and **Filters** area on the left-hand side of the form window and select **Amount** and **Lead Source** from the **Opportunities** queried dataset:

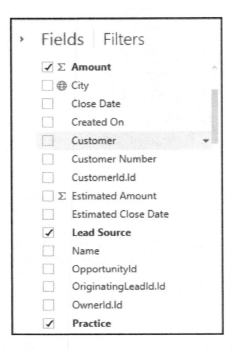

3. Change the chart type using the floating menu icon located on the left-hand side corner of the chart or the main menu chart icon located in the selection area:

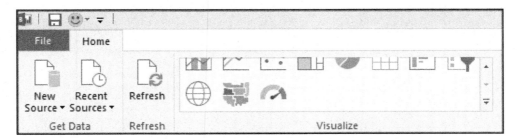

4. To resize the chart, select and drag any side or corner of the chart area.

5. Verify that the **Values, Legend,** and **Details** fields are correct by navigating to the **Fields** and **Filters** area located on the right-hand side of the Power BI window:

Table

Sometimes, all you need to see in a report is data in a tabular form. For our sales productivity dashboard, we need to add another report page and add a simple table for **Lost Deals by Territory**.

With the data in this table, we will be able to see the sales revenue numbers lost by **Product Type in a Territory**. This report will be very helpful for a sales team to see the territories that may need more attention in selling a specific product:

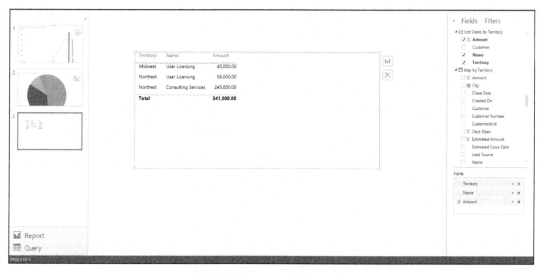

Table Product type by Territory

Using the same approach as before, create a new page and add the queried fields. This time, we will use the **Lost Deals by Territory** dataset that we created in *Chapter 3, Building Summaries and Custom Calculations*, as the source.

Here is how it is done:

1. Add a new page to your report for **Table**, navigate to the top main menu, and select **New Page**.

2. Navigate to the **Fields** and **Filters** area on the left-hand side of the form window and select **Territory**, **Amount**, and **Name** from the **Lost Deals by Territory** queried dataset:

3. Change the chart type using the floating menu icon 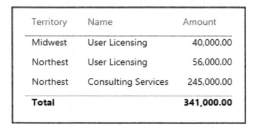 located on the left-hand side of the chart or the main menu chart icon located in the selection area.

Territory	Name	Amount
Midwest	User Licensing	40,000.00
Northest	User Licensing	56,000.00
Northest	Consulting Services	245,000.00
Total		**341,000.00**

4. To resize the chart, select and drag any side or corner of the chart area.

5. Verify the order of **Fields** by navigating to the **Fields** and **Filters** area located on the right-hand side of the Power BI window:

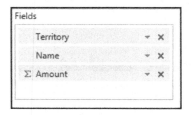

The cluster column chart

So far, we have added basic charts and tables with the Dynamics CRM queried dataset. Now, let's add a little more substance with a clustered column chart based on the pivoted sales dataset.

> In general, column charts are great to measure sales revenue. They are probably the commonly used visualization in Excel and Dynamics product lines.

With this chart, we should be able to see the sales revenue numbers split up across the individual practices by **Sales Stage**. This report will be very helpful to see the holistic view of the sales performance across each practice:

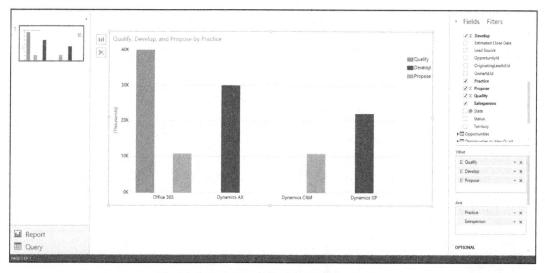

Cluster Column Chart Pipeline Phase by Practice

For our sales productivity dashboard, we need to add a new report with a cluster column chart that shows **Practice Revenue by Sales Stage**.

Here is how it is done:

1. Add a new page to your report for **Cluster Column Chart**, navigate to the top main menu, and select **New Page**.

2. Navigate to the **Fields** and **Filters** area on the left-hand side of the form window and select **Develop**, **Propose**, **Practice**, and **Salesperson** from the **Open Revenue by Sales Stage** queried dataset:

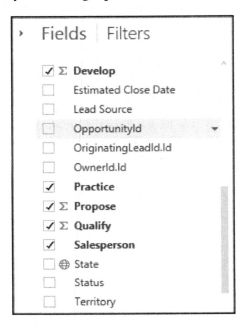

3. Change the chart type using the floating menu icon located on the left-hand side of the chart or the main menu chart icon located in the selection area:

4. To resize the chart, select and drag any side or corner of the chart area.

5. Verify the order of **Fields** by navigating to the **Fields** and **Filters** area located on the right-hand side of the Power BI window. For this chart, the fields pivoted and aggregated are based on the sales process stage, so make sure that they are in the correct order:

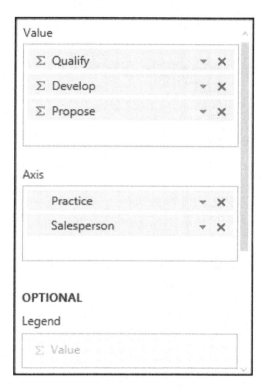

The clustered bar chart

Depending on how you want to look at the data, sometimes turning the chart in a horizontal position can uncover new information or at least expose an alternative method to a salesperson.

For our sales productivity dashboard, we need to display **Actual Revenue, and Estimated Revenue by Customer** in a single stacked bar chart. Combining two aggregated revenue fields to a single bar chart can help sales see a single view of their top customer and potential sales:

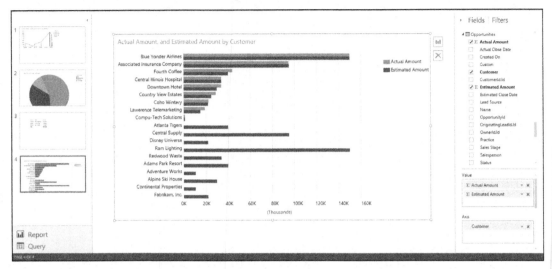

Clustered Bar Chart Estimated vs. Actual Amounts

For our sales productivity dashboard, we need to add a new report with a stacked bar chart that shows **Estimated Revenue** and **Actual Revenue** by Customer.

Here is how it is done:

1. Add a new page to your report for **Table**, navigate to the top main menu, and select **New Page**.

2. Navigate to the **Fields** and **Filters** area on the left-hand side of the form window and select **Actual Amount, Customer**, and **Estimated Amount** from the **Opportunities** queried dataset:

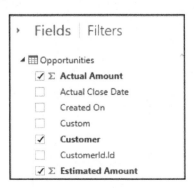

3. Change the chart type using the floating menu icon  located on the left-hand side of the chart or the main menu chart icon located in the selection area:

4. To resize the chart, select and drag any side or corner of the chart area.

5. Verify the order of **Fields** by navigating to the **Fields** and **Filters** area located on the right-hand side of the Power BI window. As we will display two-aggravated values in one **Clustered Bar Chart**, we need to make sure that the order is correct for the **Estimated Amount** and **Actual Amount** values:

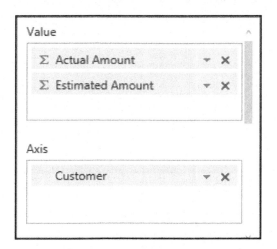

The filled map

Geographical visualization with maps is one of the newest reporting options sales teams are using to analyze data. Out of the box, Power BI provides interactive Geo-Map visualization options supported by Bing Maps.

Just like Dynamics CRM 2015 leverages Bing Maps to search the account and contact location based on address fields, so does Power BI Maps.

If a field in a queries dataset is an address type field, such as city, state, zip code, county, or country, it will automatically be resolved by Bing maps and return the geo-fence latitude and longitude without any user input.

There are two types of maps visualization in the Power BI Designer. The Bubble Map is a global 3D display and the filled map is a flat display.

With the filled map, we will be able to see the sales revenue numbers by each state and city. Using a report like this will be instrumental in expanding a sales team. Later, we will connect the practice and salesperson data to this map, displaying a deeper reporting metric for sales revenue by location (imagine the possibilities of entering a new geographical market):

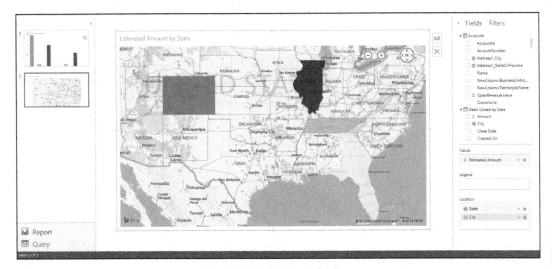

Map Estimated Amount by State

To get started, we need to add a new report with the **Filled Map** type to show **Practice(s) Revenue by State and City**.

Here is how it is done:

1. Add a new page to your report for **Table**, navigate to the top main menu, and select **New Page**.

2. Navigate to the **Fields** and **Filters** area on the left-hand side of the
    form window and select **City**, **State**, and **Estimated Amount** from the
    Opportunities queried dataset:

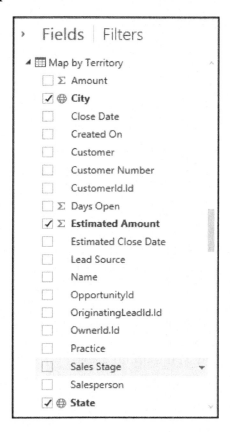

3. Change the chart type using the floating menu icon located on the left-
    side of the chart or the main menu chart icon in the selection area:

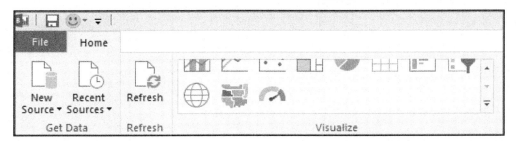

4. To resize the chart, select and drag any side or corner of the chart area.

5. Verify the order of **Fields** by navigating to the **Fields** and **Filters** area located on the right-hand side of the Power BI window:

Cards

Usually, seeing your sales data in the flat format is all you need to be productive. Out of the box, Power BI provides a basic card visualization option, which does just what it says. For a majority of salespersons, it is a very effective way to just see your data.

For our sales productivity dashboard, we need to display **Estimated Revenue** and **Customer with Number of Days the Deal is Open** in a single card. Adding customer revenue cards can help sales see a simple view of the top customer and potential sales to help with most important deals:

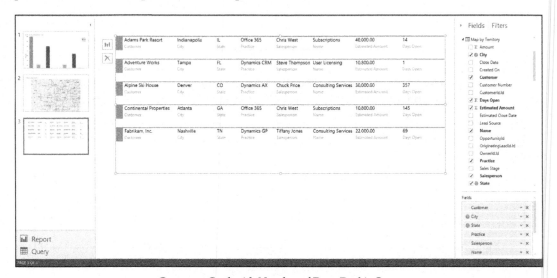

Customer Card with Number of Days Deal is Open

To get started, we need to add a new report with a **Card** type to show customer cards with the sales pipeline information with **Days Open**.

Here is how it is done:

1. Add a new page to your report for **Cards**, navigate to the top main menu, and select **New Page.**

2. Navigate to the **Fields** and **Filters** area on the left-hand side of the form window and select **City**, **State**, **Customer**, **Days Open**, **Name**, **Salesperson**, **Practice**, and **Estimated Amount** from the **Opportunities** queried dataset:

3. Change the chart type using the floating menu icon ⊞ located on the left-hand side of the chart or the main menu chart icon ⊟ located in the selection area:

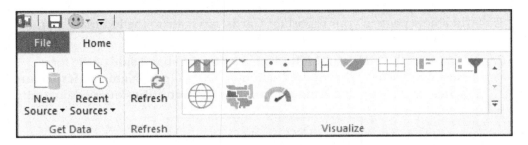

4. To resize the chart, select and drag any side or corner of the chart area.

5. Verify the order of **Fields** by navigating to the **Fields** and **Filters** area located on the right-hand side of the Power BI window:

Putting it all together

Viewing each chart, cards, and map on a separate report page may make it easier to design, update, and/or troubleshoot your charts, maps, and/or tables, but at some point, we may want to have a single page with everything on it. This is as simple as copy and paste.

In *Chapter 6*, *Adding ERP Data*, when we upload these reports to the Power BI for the Office 365 site, every report page will be loaded. So, either way, all the charts, maps, cards, and tables will be available for a user to view:

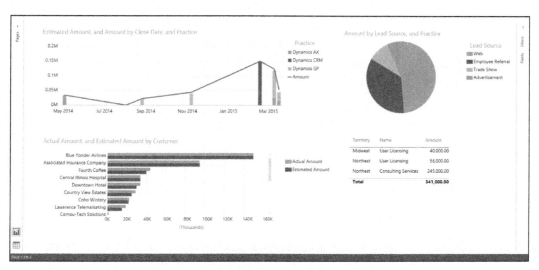

All reports together in the Sales Productivity Report

If you do want to add all the seven charts and maps to one or two report pages, it is as simple as copy and paste; here is a simple example of how to do it:

1. Select a report page and individual chart, map, or table.
2. Use *Ctl+C* to copy the chart, map, or table.
3. Use *Ctl+V* on the new report page to paste the chart, map, or table.
4. To resize each chart, select and drag any side or corner of the chart area.

To add another report page for all other charts, follow the same process. Here is an example of how to use map and cards on the same report. Simple as that…

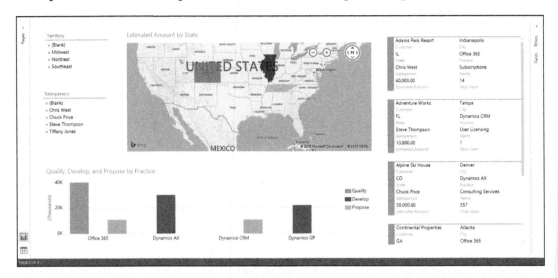

Summary

In this chapter, we reviewed seven different visualization types to use in the reports, including charts, maps, cards, and tables. We also verified the field placement on the charts and maps and added all the seven charts and maps to just two report pages with a simple copy and paste.

In the next chapter, we will enhance the clarity of the charts and maps by adding filters, slicers, and timelines based on territory, practice, and salespersons.

5

Enhance Data Clarity Using Filters and Slicers

So far, we have made a lot of progress building a really sharp report for our sales productivity dashboard with a variety of different visualizations. Now, let's keep it going and add a bit of interactivity. At the end of the day, what would a dashboard be if you could not carve up the data the way you wanted to see it?

The Power BI Designer and Power BI for Office 365 provides a native functionality to create a truly interactive user experience in order to analyze the report data. In this chapter, you will learn the basics of how to add the interactive querying functionality to the reports, using a variety of different data filters and slicers.

We need to prepare the reports for presentation in the sales productivity dashboard by sorting our top customer revenue, making sure **Lost Products by Territory** only displays the deals that we lost. Next, we should be able to look at the deals closed real time by year, quarter, and/or month. Lastly, add the interactive data manipulation based on any combination of territory and/or salespersons in a list selection.

We will cover scenarios of how to perform this with the following methods:

- Sort and drill down
- Add a column filter
- Apply visualization filters
- Add view filters
- Create custom slicers

Filtering your data

Being able to filter data is essential to any dashboard. With Power BI, data can be filtered in a variety of different ways with data columns, report pages, individual charts, tables, and/or maps. We can also add data slicers to all the report pages that will allow even more real-time interaction.

The best thing about Power BI is that it has a lot of features built-in already to filter the report data. If you simply select a chart or map on a report page, the values and visualizations on the rest of the page will change, as shown in the following screenshot:

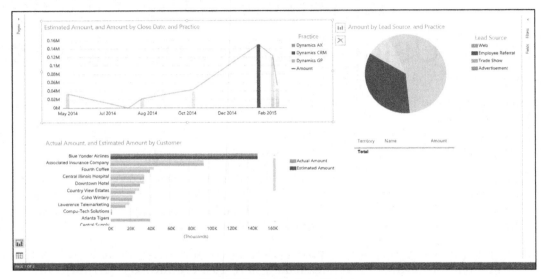

Filtered Sales Productivity Report

This works in Power BI because all the visualizations are already connected based on either the automatic relationship detection and/or the merged and combined relationship that we created in *Chapter 2, Organizing and Consolidating Dynamics CRM 2015 Datasets*. How cool is that?

 With the Power BI Designer and Power BI for Office 365, the automatic data detection is enabled and will run on the initial load of datasets. The detection works for a variety of data sources, such as text, CSV, database, web service, and so on, in the Power BI Designer and Power BI for Office 365.

To add a little more, there are additional built-in features, such as fly-outs, drilldowns, and sorting, available on every report for even more real-time interaction.

Here are a few examples of these features:

Fly-out

A really easy option for real-time filtering is to just hover over a visualization on a report page. When you hover over an area of the chart or map, a fly-out display will appear with details on the selected area data.

Here is an example of a fly-out on the **Amount by Lead Source, and Practice** pie chart. This fly-out shows the total amount of revenue from web leads for **Practice: Dynamics GP**:

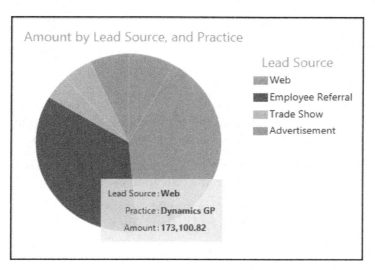

Drill down

If the fly-out does not give us the information we need and if we want to get a little deeper into the data, we can drill down from within a chart or map. Drill downs only work if the visualization contains a hierarchy. If it does, we can drill down by double-clicking on an area to see the next level of detail. The **Qualify, Develop, and Propose** bar graph visualization has a hierarchy made up of **Practice** and **Salesperson**; each **Practice** has one or more salespersons.

Here is an example of a drill down in a visualization with the **Qualify, Develop, and Propose** bar graph from **Practice** to **Salesperson**:

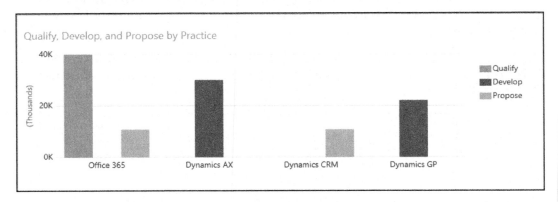

By default, the **Qualify, Develop, and Propose** bar graph displays only the **Practice** data because **Practice** appears in the axis bucket before **Salesperson**.

1. To drill down to **Salesperson**, double-click on one of the chart bars. The data in the bar graph will change to the **Salesperson** view:

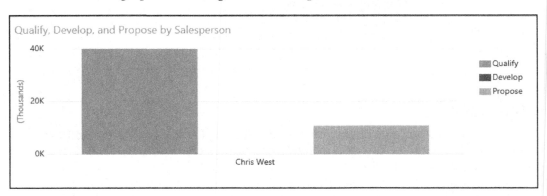

2. To return to a preceding level, right-click on the visualization and select the up arrow icon, , from the menu:

Sort

What if you need to sort your data in a chart or table? No need to go back to the original dataset to do this. The sorting the data option is available in most charts and can be very useful to see data in a different view very quickly.

For example, in the **Actual Amount and Estimated Amount by Customer** horizontal bar chart, we need to make sure that **Estimated Revenue** is ordered from greatest to least (top to bottom).

Here is an example of how you sort by actual revenue descending in the bar chart:

1. Click on the empty space inside the **Actual Amount and Estimated Amount by Customer** visualization to show the menu:

2. Once the menu appears, select **Sort by** to open the drop-down arrow and then select **Actual Amount**:

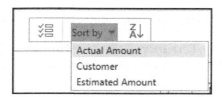

3. To sort the data in the chart, click on the **AZ** icon to switch between ascending and descending. We want to see the data in a descending order:

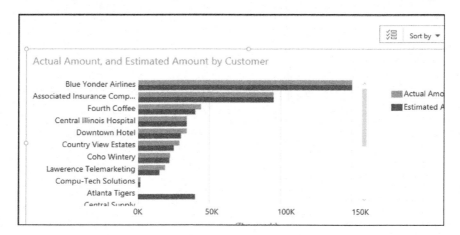

Adding filters to the data

Most of the time, the built-in filtering can get the job done, but for our reports, we need to take it a step further. We need to add additional filters to the charts, maps, and tables that allow you to view data by a time frame or status. By adding the **Column** and **DateTime** filters to our datasets, we can eliminate unneeded records to report. Let's take a look at a few examples.

The column filter

A lot of CRM systems may have data that you never want to pull to your dashboard. This data needs to get filtered from the dataset before it is presented in a report. By adding different column filters to our underlining dataset, we can accomplish this.

 Using column filters can also help with the overall performance of the reports by limiting the amount of data sent to the report.

A great example is to add a filter to the **Status** column in our **Deals Lost by Territory** dataset. For this chart, we only need to show **Deals** that have the status as **Lost**.

Here is how we add a column filter to this dataset:

1. In the **Lost Deals by Territory** dataset in the query view window, select the **Status** column, check the **Lost** option from the menu, and click on **OK**:

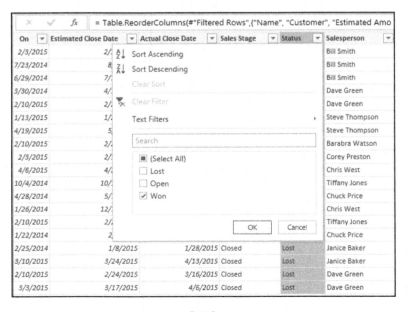

2. Once the dataset finishes refreshing, you will only see data with the status as **Lost**:

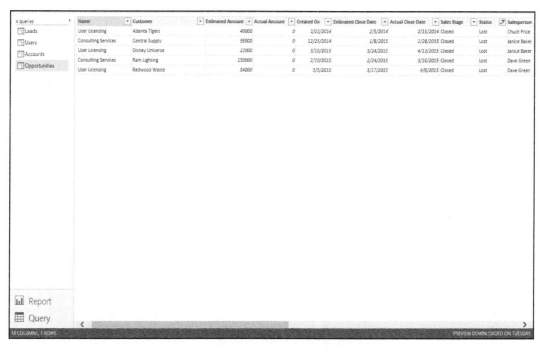

Lost Opportunities Query View

3. Now, use the same process for each dataset with the following list for reference:

   ° Deals by Lead Source (Status = Won)
   ° Deals Closed by Date (Status = Won)
   ° Map by Territory (Status = Open)
   ° Open Revenue by Sales Stage (Status = Open)

The DateTime filter

Another popular option to filter data is date and time. As part of the sample opportunities data that we imported, we added a few opportunity records from 2010 that we do not want to include in our reports. This deal may be real, so we may not want to delete them from the Dynamics CRM.

A built-in **DateTime** filter is included with Power BI. We can use this filter to eliminate these unneeded opportunities.

We can use the following options with the **DateTime** filter to adjust the date and/or time:

- Today
- This week
- This month
- This quarter
- Year to Date
- Custom

Here is an example of how it's done in the **Opportunities** dataset:

1. In **Query View**, select the **Opportunities** dataset and the **Created On** column and then select **Date Filters | Custom Filter**:

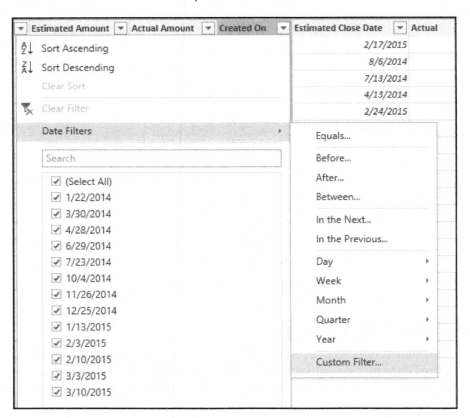

2. Once the **Filter Rows** window appears, select **is after or equal to** from the drop-down menu and add the date as **1/1/2014**:

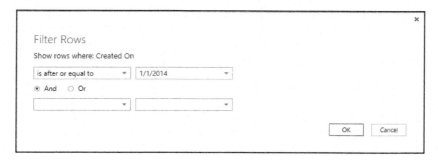

Remember in *Chapter 3, Building Summaries and Custom Calculations,* we created an individual dataset by duplicating the opportunities dataset to use with each example. Review each of those datasets to make sure that this **DateTime** filter is applied in the same way so that all the report data is correctly displayed in each visualization.

Report filters

There are two main types of report filters. The **Visualization** filter or the chart-level filter applies to each individual visualization on the report page. The **View** filter or the page-level filter applies to the entire report page and all the visualizations on the page.

Interacting with report filters

The methods to interact with reports are **Reading View** and **Editing View.** Each one has different filtering capabilities available, which depend on which mode you're in.

In the **Editing View**, you can add the page filter and the visualization filter. When you save the report, these filters are saved with it.

In the **Reading View**, you can interact with the filters you added, but you cannot save their changes. In this view, you can also interact with any page and visualization filters that already exist in the report, but you won't be able to save your filter changes.

Visualization filters — charts, tables, or maps

As mentioned at the beginning of the chapter, the actual charts, tables, and maps themselves can be used as filters by just selecting a visualization. Having said that, once a visualization is added to a report page, it also becomes a selectable filter option under **Fields | Filters** on the right-hand side of the report page view. At any time, you can select an individual chart, map, or table, and these flters are available.

Let's take a look at the **Amount by Lead Source and Practice** pie chart as an example.

1. In the **Amount by Lead Source and Practice** pie chart located on the **Organization Review** report page, select the **Filters** link located in the upper-right corner of the window:

2. Under **Filters**, navigate to the **CHART** link; you will see the filters that you just added for **Amount**, **Lead Source**, and **Practice**:

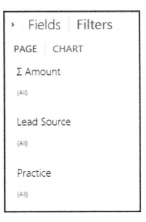

3. Under the **Practice** filter list, select **Dynamics CRM** and **Dynamics AX** from the list:

4. Calculated Σ type filters operate a little differently than other filters. You will be presented with several drop-down options to add querying statements. Select **Amount**, set the calculated filter option to **is less than**, and enter **50000**:

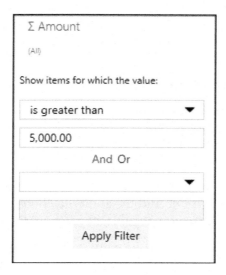

5. Return to the report page to verify that the chart only displays the **Lead Source** totals for the Dynamics CRM revenue that is greater than **50000** and then click on **Apply Filter**:

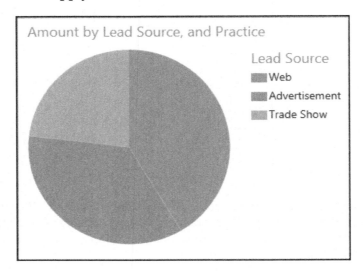

6. To clear the filters, select the filter icon, ⧩, on the individual filter list or make sure that all the filter sections are unchecked.

Using the page filter

Visualization filters are great, but it can be a lot of work if you have multiple charts and maps on a single report page that you need to keep up with. It would be great to be able to create a global filter for the entire report page and for every visualization on it. Well, you can.

Let's take the example of a sales executive who may need the ability to review the data based on a certain time frame and the ability to choose a filter value without having to adjust each individual chart, table, or map on the report page.

This **Organizational Review** report page contains three different charts and one table that we want to be able to filter by: **Year**, **Quarter**, and **Month**. In *Chapter 3, Building Summaries and Custom Calculations*, we already created these columns, so now let's use them.

To add the **View** filter to the **Organizational Review** report page, we need to follow the same process as the **Visualization Filter**, but this time, add the page filter type to the entire page.

Here is how you do it:

1. On the **Organization Review** report page, select **Fields | Filters** in the upper-right corner.

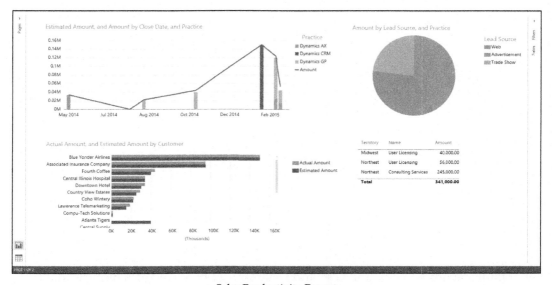

Sales Productivity Report

2. Highlight the **Fields** heading and drag the **Year**, **Quarter**, and **Month** fields from the **Opportunities** dataset to the **Filters** heading:

3. Once all the fields are added, navigate to the **PAGE** link under **Fields |
Filters**, select **Year** as **2015** and **Quarter** as **1**, and review the report page:

By default, each field value for **Year** and **Quarter** will be stored as a numeric data
type. If you use the **Month** date type and need to see the actual name value, use the
process you learned in *Chapter 2, Organizing and Consolidating Dynamics CRM 2015
Datasets*, to change the column type to text and then replace the value with the actual
name of the month.

Adding slicers

Using filters is a nice way to carve up the report data, but to give users the ability
to review scenarios the way they want to write on the report itself could be a better
option. Filters can be applied to Power BI-queried datasets, report pages, and
individual report visualizations, but a slicer is a chart type that is only used on
individual report pages.

For example, a sales manager using the **Sales Revenue** report may want to view the data by **Practice** and **Salesperson** in different scenarios directly from the report page to ensure that the results are meaningful. Slicers are the best option for this.

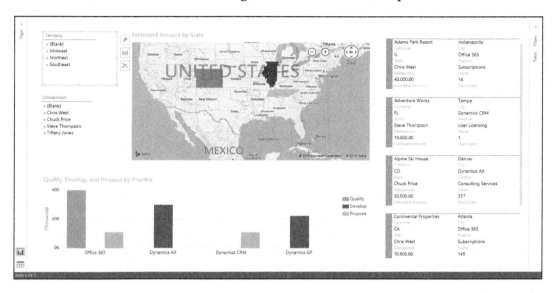

Here is how we add slicers for **Territory** and **Salesperson** to the **Sales Revenue** report:

1. On a **Sales Revenue** report page, drag the **Territory** field from the **Map Revenue** dataset (located under **Fields | Filters**) to the report.

2. Next, change the type of visualization to slicer by selecting the filter icon, in the main menu or the quick menu by right-clicking on the visualization.

3. Once the visualization changes to slicer, you will have a selectable list of territories to choose from to filter the report data:

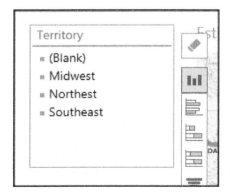

4. Repeat the process with the **Salesperson** field in the same dataset:

Salesperson

- (Blank)
- Chris West
- Chuck Price
- Steve Thompson
- Tiffany Jones

5. To clear all the slicer sections, right-click on the slicer and then select the quick menu icon, ▨.

By default, these slicers, charts, maps, and tables on the report page are already connected because the relationship between the datasets is already established.

Summary

In this chapter, we discovered how to automatically, merge and/or combine dataset relationships are built-in without any manual process. We discussed how to interact with filters and slicers on a report page. We also looked at how to sort data on the fly and adjust timeline parameters.

In *Chapter 6, Adding ERP Data*, we will connect to an external ERP data source and combine our Dynamics CRM 2015 sales data with
the ERP financial data to provide a 360 degree view of the organization. Once we have the data connected, we will create a new report, which is aimed at visualizing a customer's health.

6
Adding ERP Data

Having all your Dynamics CRM data in a nice and easy-to-use report is great, but what if we wanted to add a little bit more by combining the sales data with the ERP billing data together on the same report?

Let's say that the management wants to see the sales pipeline information compared to the actual amount due and what type of paying customer they are. This may shed some light on how the customer is actually looking compared to estimating.

In this chapter, you will learn how to combine the Dynamics CRM and ERP information by:

- Adding a new ERP data source
- Joining data between CRM and ERP
- Building a combined **Customer Health** report

Getting started

The Power BI Designer and Power BI for Office 365 contain a variety of different data source connectors that we can use to access the data of ERP. A few of these options are:

- SQL Server
- ODBC
- SSAS Connector for Dynamics GP Analysis Cubes

In this chapter, we will use the connector for SQL Server, which is a deployed instance of SQL Server databases for the Dynamics GP sample company database. If you do not have access to a Dynamics GP instance, download and import the sample TWO.mdf database file from the following link (https://www.dropbox. com/s/e3ohgpz8agtxc7h/TWO.mdf?dl=0). If you have Dynamics GP installed with the sample company, use the TWO database.

To download a trail version of the latest version of SQL Server, refer to `http://www.microsoft.com/en-us/evalcenter/evaluate-sql-server-2014`.

Dynamics GP deployment

The Dynamics GP application is deployed using a local installation of SQL Server, so we will have to configure Power BI to connect to the On-Premise environment. Since Power BI is a web-based tool, this means that we will need to connect and authenticate to the actual SQL Server that is installed on a local server.

In this chapter, we will launch the Power BI Designer and Power BI for the Office 365 site while they are authenticated to the same network as the Dynamics GP instance to build our new ERP datasets. To build the new ERP dataset, we first have to connect to SQL Server and the TWO database and then initiate a query-based SQL script.

Here is an example of how the sample data from the TWO database will look in Dynamics GP if you have it installed. If you do not have Dynamics GP installed, the imported TWO database is all you need.

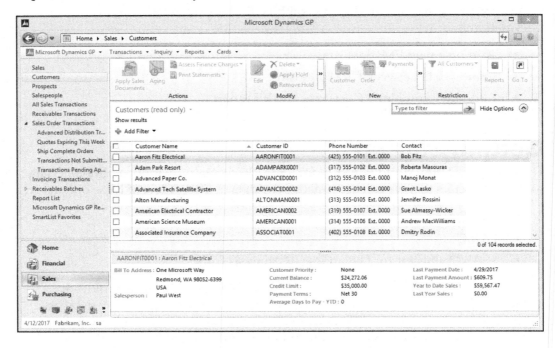

The customer aging script

With a customer aging query script, we can build the perfect customer health report that joins the Dynamics CRM sales data and the Dynamics GP ERP data, as shown in the following screenshot:

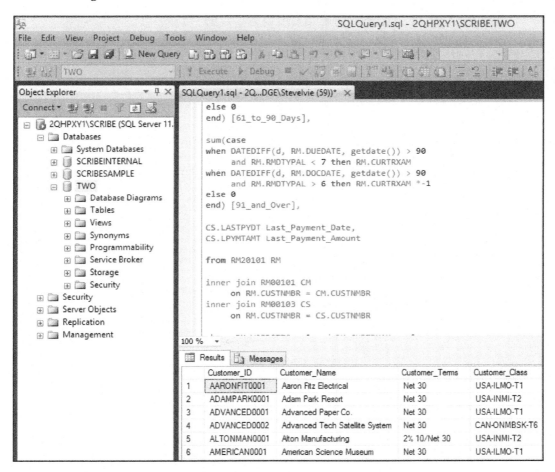

One of the most popular queries to view Dynamics GP customer aging is *Vitoria Yudin's, Current Receivables Aging Summary* query that shows one row per customer with a balance and hard-coded aging buckets aged by due date:

```
select
CM.CUSTNMBR Customer_ID, CM.CUSTNAME Customer_Name,
CM.PYMTRMID Customer_Terms, CM.CUSTCLAS Customer_Class,
CM.PRCLEVEL Price_Level,
```

```
sum(case
when RM.RMDTYPAL < 7 then RM.CURTRXAM
else RM.CURTRXAM * -1
end) Total_Due,

sum(case
when DATEDIFF(d, RM.DUEDATE, getdate()) < 31
      and RM.RMDTYPAL < 7 then RM.CURTRXAM
when DATEDIFF(d, RM.DOCDATE, getdate()) < 31
      and RM.RMDTYPAL > 6 then RM.CURTRXAM *-1
else 0
end) [Current],

sum(case
when DATEDIFF(d, RM.DUEDATE, getdate()) between 31 and 60
      and RM.RMDTYPAL < 7 then RM.CURTRXAM
when DATEDIFF(d, RM.DOCDATE, getdate()) between 31 and 60
      and RM.RMDTYPAL > 6 then RM.CURTRXAM * -1
else 0
end) [31_to_60_Days],

sum(case
when DATEDIFF(d, RM.DUEDATE, getdate()) between 61 and 90
      and RM.RMDTYPAL < 7 then RM.CURTRXAM
when DATEDIFF(d, RM.DOCDATE, getdate()) between 61 and 90
      and RM.RMDTYPAL > 6 then RM.CURTRXAM * -1
else 0
end) [61_to_90_Days],

sum(case
when DATEDIFF(d, RM.DUEDATE, getdate()) > 90
      and RM.RMDTYPAL < 7 then RM.CURTRXAM
when DATEDIFF(d, RM.DOCDATE, getdate()) > 90
      and RM.RMDTYPAL > 6 then RM.CURTRXAM *-1
else 0
end) [91_and_Over],

CS.LASTPYDT Last_Payment_Date,
CS.LPYMTAMT Last_Payment_Amount

from RM20101 RM

inner join RM00101 CM
      on RM.CUSTNMBR = CM.CUSTNMBR
inner join RM00103 CS
      on RM.CUSTNMBR = CS.CUSTNMBR
```

```
where RM.VOIDSTTS = 0 and RM.CURTRXAM <> 0

group by CM.CUSTNMBR, CM.CUSTNAME, CM.PYMTRMID, CM.CUSTCLAS,
        CM.PRCLEVEL, CS.LASTPYDT,CS.LPYMTAMT
```

The preceding query can also be found at `http://victoriayudin.com/2012/01/25/sql-view-for-current-receivables-aging-in-dynamics-gp/`.

Getting new data

Figuring out how to access and authenticate to a SQL Server environment from Power BI can be a cumbersome process, but once we have established that access, we can begin building the ERP datasets in Power BI.

Let's take a look at an example of how we connect to SQL Server using the Power BI Designer:

1. In the **Query View** window, select **Get Data** from the **Home** tab under the top menu and select the **SQL Server** option:

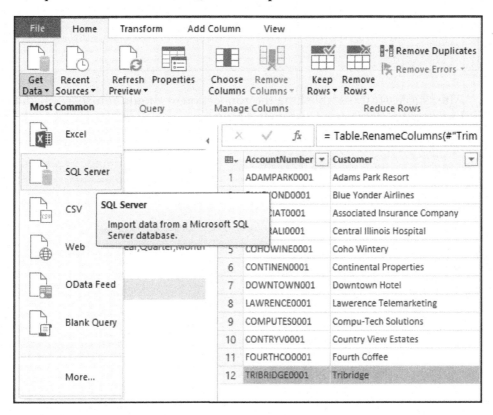

2. Using the **Microsoft SQL Server** import window, enter the Server name as DYNSE and the Database name as TWO, add the **Customer Aging** query, and click on **OK**:

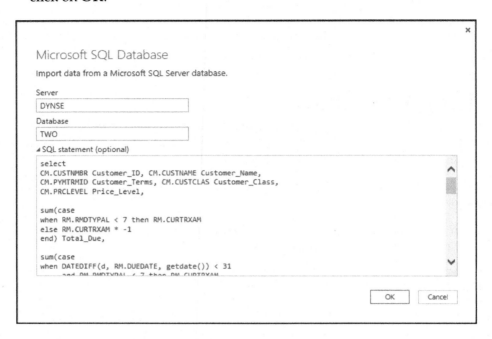

3. After successfully establishing the connection, it should return a new dataset. Rename this dataset as **Customer Aging**:

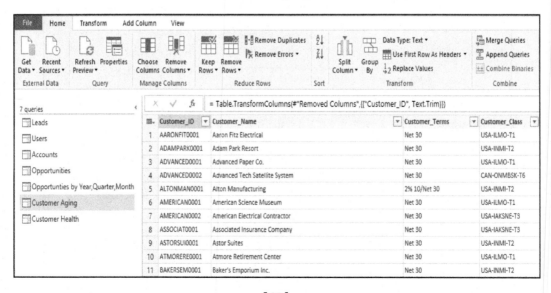

Joining customer aging

For our customer health report, we need to create a single dataset that combines the sale pipeline information with the customer aging information.

Here is how we join the datasets:

1. Create a copy of the **Accounts** dataset and rename **Customer Health**.

2. In the **Query View** window, update the data type to text for both columns: **AccountNumber** and **Customer_ID** in the **Customer Aging** and **Customer Health** datasets.

3. Staying in the **Query View** window, select **Format | Trim** from the **Transform** tab under the main menu to ensure that there are no extra spaces in the **AccountNumber** and **Customer_ID** columns:

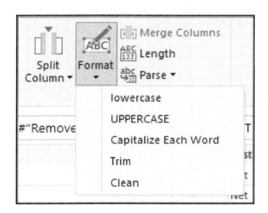

4. Select the **Merge Columns** tab under the **Transform** menu tab at the top of the **Query View** window. Merge the dataset with **AccountNumber** and **Customer_ID**:

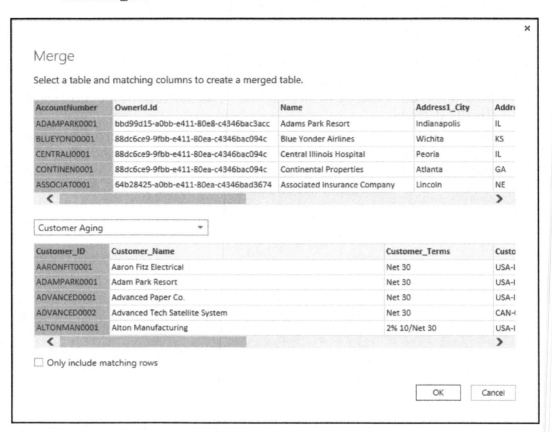

5. After the merging process is complete, we will see the **Dynamics GP Customer Aging** information alongside the **Account Sales** information from **Dynamics CRM**:

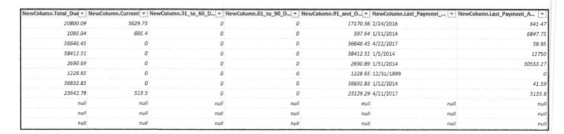

Building the report

With the new dataset in place, we can now build the **Customer Health** report to include in our sales productivity dashboard. Following the same process that we performed in *Chapter 4, Improving the Look and Feel by Adding Charts, Tables, and Maps*, we will add visualization from the combined **Customer Health** dataset to build a new report page. This is an example of the report we want to create, but some of the graphs we need are not ready yet, so we will need to build them:

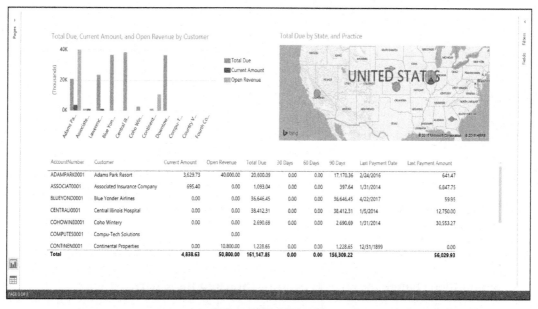

Customer Health Report

At the end of the day, we want to add a report that shows us the sales pipeline information compared with the actual outstanding amount to get a 360 degree view of a customer. We can see this information by adding a chart, map, and table to a new report.

Take a look at the following examples for:

- **Total due, Current Amount and Open Revenue** bar chart
- **Total Due By State** and **Practice Map**
- **Sales** and **Billing Table**

Before we add the new visualizations to the **Customer Health** report, update the dataset value names by navigating to **Field | Filters** on the left-hand side of the **Report View** window and select **Rename** from the drop-down menu link:

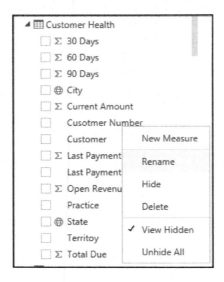

Now that the **Customer Health** dataset is renamed, here is how we add the visualizations:

1. Using the **Customer Health** dataset in the **Report View** window, select **Total Due, Current Amount, Open Revenue** values and **Customer** as axis and then change the chart type to 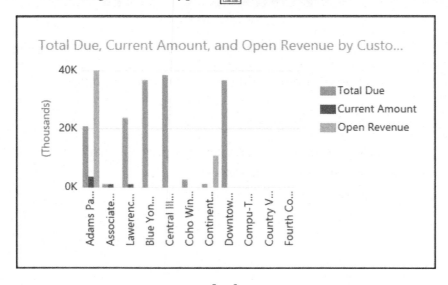 **Stacked Bar Chart**:

2. Using the **Customer Health** dataset in the **Report View** window, select **Total Due** values as **State, City** as **Location**, and **Practice** as **Legend** and then change the chart type to ⊕ **Map**:

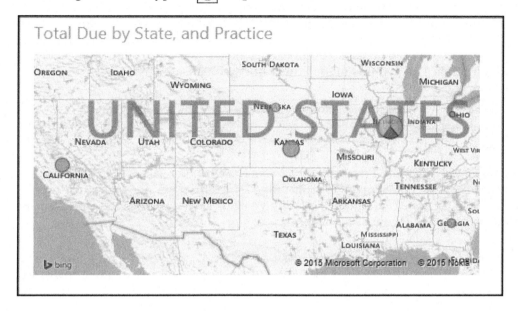

3. Using the **Customer Health** dataset in the **Query View** window, select **AccountNumber, Customer, Open Revenue, Current Amount, Total Amount, 30 Days, 60 Days, 90 Days, Last Payment Date, Last Payment Amount** and then change the chart type to ▦ **Table**:

AccountNumber	Customer	Current Amount	Open Revenue	Total Due	30 Days	60 Days	90 Days	Last Payment Date	Last Payment Amount
ADAMPARK0001	Adams Park Resort	3,629.73	40,000.00	20,800.09	0.00	0.00	17,170.36	2/24/2016	641.47
ASSOCIAT0001	Associated Insurance Company	695.40	0.00	1,093.04	0.00	0.00	397.64	1/31/2014	6,847.75
BLUEYOND0001	Blue Yonder Airlines	0.00	0.00	36,646.45	0.00	0.00	36,646.45	4/22/2017	59.95
CENTRALI0001	Central Illinois Hospital	0.00	0.00	38,412.31	0.00	0.00	38,412.31	1/5/2014	12,750.00
COHOWINE0001	Coho Wintery	0.00	0.00	2,690.69	0.00	0.00	2,690.69	1/31/2014	30,553.27
COMPUTES0001	Compu-Tech Solutions	0.00							
CONTINEN0001	Continental Properties	0.00	10,800.00	1,228.65	0.00	0.00	1,228.65	12/31/1899	0.00
Total		**4,838.63**	**50,800.00**	**161,147.85**	**0.00**	**0.00**	**156,309.22**		**56,029.93**

Accessing the ERP data from the cloud

Most ERP systems are deployed on-premise with an actual local database. These are accessible by tools, such as the Power BI Designer, but what if we want to access the On-Premise database from the cloud-based Power BI site for Office 365? This means that before we are able to access any data from an Office 365 site, we need to install and configure secured access to our local machine or server from the Office 365 site in the cloud. We do just this in the Power BI Personal Gateway.

> For additional information on the Power BI Personal Gateway, refer to `https://support.powerbi.com/knowledgebase/articles/649846`.

In *Chapter 7, Deploy and Present Reports to the Power BI Site*, you will learn how to upload and view your Power BI report file to the Office 365 site. With the Power BI Personal Gateway configured, it will give us the way to access the On-Premise database from the cloud.

Here is how you configure the gateway:

1. From the Office 365 for the Power BI site, we need to download **Power BI Personal Gateway** by navigating to the top-right corner and selecting the download link:

2. Once you have the personal gateway downloaded, select the location, click on **Next** to install, and follow the configuration process:

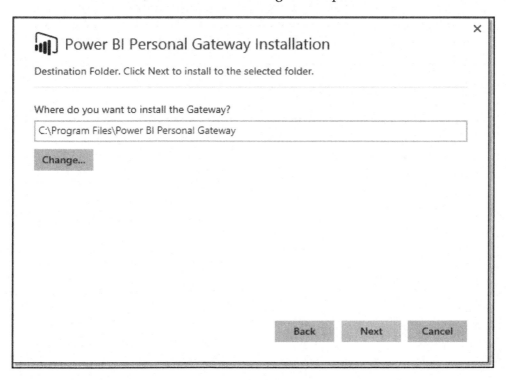

3. After you have installed and configured the gateway location, sign in to your Power BI site by selecting the **Next** button or the **Sign in to Power BI** link with the same credentials that you used to log in to the Power BI site:

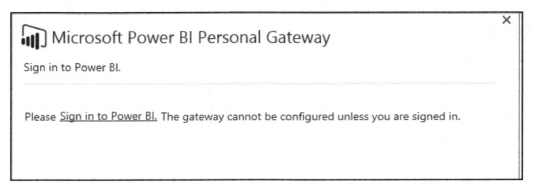

4. Now that you are successfully signed in to the Power BI site, you have to enter your credentials for your local environment with `<DOMAIN or MACHINE>\<USER`. These credentials need to have rights to the machine that you have installed the Personal Gateway on. Also, as we will use a SQL Server, the user credentials should have read access to that as well.

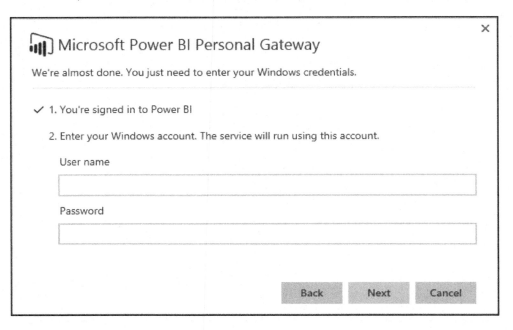

After configuring our Power BI site to connect to our On-Premise environment with the **Power BI Personal Gateway**, we can connect to any local data source as long as the machine is online.

Summary

In this chapter, you learned how to combine datasets from Dynamics CRM and Dynamics GP to build a combined **Customer Health** report, showing a 360 degree view of the sales pipeline information and the actual customer receivables that is outstanding. Using the techniques you learned in *Chapter 4, Improving the Look and Feel by Adding Charts, Tables, and Maps*, we added visualizations to a new report to add to our sales productivity dashboard.

In the next chapter, *Chapter 7, Deploy and Present Reports to the Power BI Site*, we will connect to Power BI for the Office 365 site and upload our Power BI **Sales Productivity** report source file to the site. Once we have the file loaded, we will share and present the information with the sales productivity dashboard.

7
Deploy and Present Reports to the Power BI Site

A common request from an executive is to see the report data in a dashboard from wherever they may be. In the past, this was a detailed process and provided minimum results. However, now with Power BI sites, we can push our newly designed reports to a prebuilt website and then share it with anyone and everyone we like.

In this chapter, you will learn how to:

- Upload the Power BI Designer file to the Power BI site
- Review Power BI for Office 365 editing
- Pin reports to the sales productivity dashboard
- Share reports with users
- Set up refreshable schedules

Power BI sites

Power BI sites for Office 365 is yet another way to build interactive reports and dashboards. Stacked with a handful of built-in connectors for the Dynamics CRM, Dynamics Marketing, and SSAS applications, it can be very useful to model data from anywhere you are. The Power BI site has lots of the same core capabilities as the Power BI Designer tool.

 There are two version of the Power BI subscription. The Base Power BI is free with any version of Office 365. Power BI Pro is an additional cost per data capacity limit. For information about the cost of Power BI, refer to https://powerbi. microsoft.com/pricing.

Power BI for Office 365 sites differs from the Power BI Designer in a few ways, but not many.

With Power BI for the Office 365 site, we can:

- Access the report and data anywhere where we can get online
- Configure the automatic report refresh schedule
- Collaborate with others on the reports and data
- Maintain a single data catalog that multiple users can build reports from
- Connect to mobile apps

To get our sales productivity reports in the Power BI site for Office 365, we need to first verify that we have access to the site.

Here is how we do this:

1. Navigate to `https://app.powerbi.com/dashboards` and enter the Office 365 username and password for your Power BI preview instance. Once you gain access to the site, you will be presented with a blank canvas to start adding reports:

Uploading the file to the Power BI site

Now that we have access to our Power BI for the Office 365 site, let's upload our sales productivity Power BI Designer file. To do this, we need to make sure that we are able to access the file locally.

Here is how you upload a Power BI Designer file to the site:

1. In the main site page window, select the **Get Data** link located in the bottom-left corner and select the **Files** option:

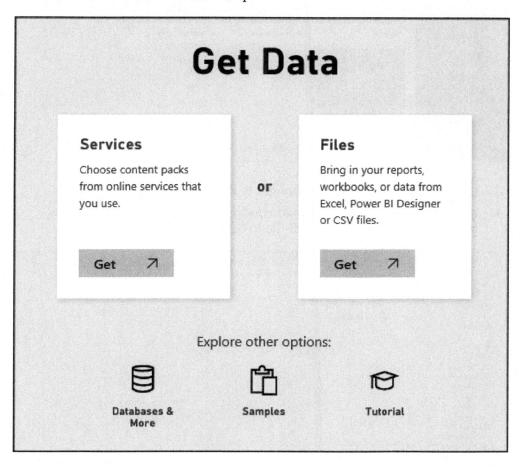

2. Once on the **Get Data** screen, select **Local File.** Files can also be stored in a **Business** or **Personal** OneDrive location:

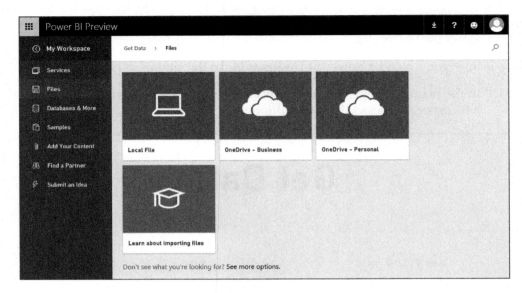

3. Once the site page window changes to the Power BI Designer file.

4. After the **Choose File to Upload** window opens, browse to the `Sales Productivity.pbix` Power BI file to begin the upload:

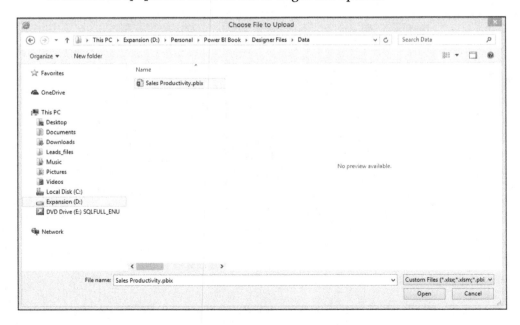

5. Once the file upload is complete, navigate back to **My Workspace** and locate the new **Sales Productivity** entries under **Dashboards**, **Reports**, and **Datasets** on the left-hand side of the site page before the **Get Data** link:

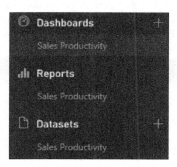

6. Select the **Reports** heading to open the first report. Open the page filters we configured in *Chapter 5, Enhance Data Clarity Using Filters and Slicers* and select **Practice**:

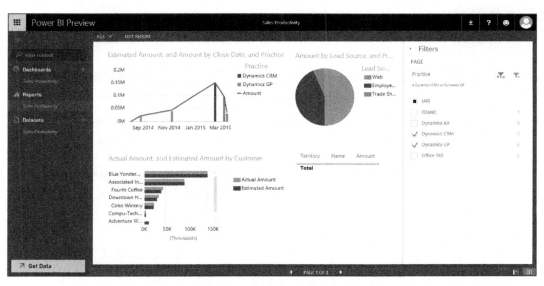

Sales Productivity Report uploaded to Office 365 Site for Power BI

Editing reports within the Power BI site

Now that we have the **Sales Productivity** reports loaded on the site, let's take a look around and see the editing options that we have. There is a column out of order on the **Sale Productivity** report with the **Customer Receivable** table on it. We need to move the **Open Revenue** column to the left-hand side of **Current Amount**.

Let's take a look at an example of how we do this by editing this report using the Power BI for the Office 365 site:

1. In the main site page window, select the **Sales Productivity** link under **Reports** on the left-hand side of the site page above the **Get Data** link. The first report page will be displayed in the window:

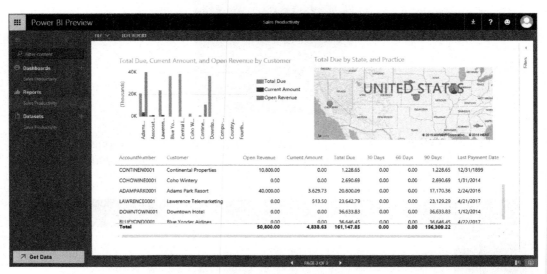

Sales Productivity Report uploaded to Power BI site with ERP information

2. In the site window, select the **EDIT REPORT** menu link from the top of the page. Once the link is selected, we will be in the equivalent of a Power BI Designer Page except now using the web version. We have the same options as the Power BI Designer tool, but now, multiple users can work on the reports together, as shown in the following screenshot:

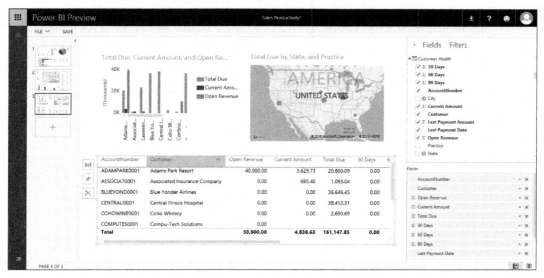

Modifying a column in Power BI site

3. Move **Open Revenue** up one spot before **Current Amount**:

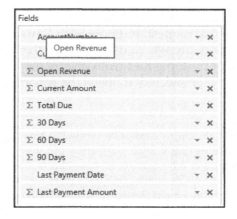

4. If there are any changes made to the reports, select **Save** from the top of the site window. If there needs to be a new copy made, select **Save As** to save a copy. This copy will be available under **Reports** on the main site page:

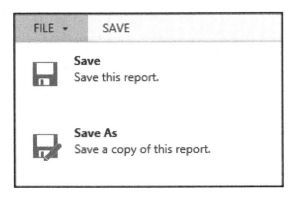

Reporting visualizations to the dashboard

Executives always want to see a single dashboard with all their data. In the past, this seemed like an impossible request, but now with Power BI for Office 365 sites, there is a self-service functionality where users can pin their report visualizations to a dashboard. We can add multiple tiles from one report or a single tile from multiple reports. When a tile is selected, it opens the report page that contains the original visualization.

> Some visualizations cannot be pinned at this time. The only visualizations that you can currently pin to a dashboard are bar, column, combo, gauge, line pie charts, cards, basics maps, scatter and bubble charts, images, tables and single card tiles. The future releases of Power BI will include more options.

For our sales productivity dashboard page, we need to pin all the supported visualizations that we have to the dashboard as tiles. After this, rename each tile as follows:

-   **Deals Closed**: This specifies **Estimated Amount, and Amount by Close Date, and Practice**

-   **Amount by Lead Source**: This denotes **Amount by Lead Source, and Practice**

- **Lost Products by Territory and Type**: This specifies **No Title**
- **Practice Pipeline by Stage**: This denotes **Qualify, Develop, and Propose by Practice**
- **Top Accounts Closed Est vs. Act**: This specifies **Actual Amount, and Estimated Amount by Customer**
- **Customer Sales List by Account Number**: This denotes **No Title**
- **Account Receivables by State and Practice**: This denotes **No Title**

Pinning a tile

There are two methods to create a tile on a dashboard page. The first is while in the reading view and the next while in the editing view. Both methods produce the same results.

Here is an example of how you do it:

1. Open the organizational review report in Power BI for Office 365, select **Estimated Amount, and Amount by Close Date, and Practice** from the **Reports** pages, and select the pin [ ] icon that will appear in the top-right corner of the visualization:

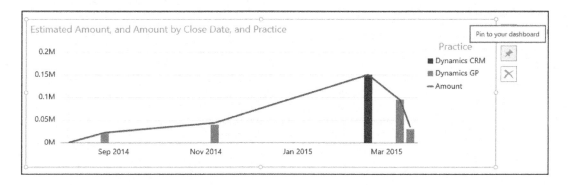

2. Continue to add all the visualization to the dashboard. We can shrink or expand the tile by selecting a corner:

Sales Productivity Dashboard on the Office 365 Power BI site

Renaming a tile

Renaming each tile to something that make sense can help users know what they are looking at. To simplify readability, add or rename each tile.

> Changes including add, delete, or update visualizations in reports will not be saved in the original Power BI Designer file. If there needs to be a change made to a Power BI Designer file, you have to use designer.

Here is an example of how we add a title to the **Lost Product by Territory** tile:

1. From the main sales productivity dashboard page in **Power BI for Office 365**, select the tile for **Lost Products by Territory**.

2. Add a new title to the tile using the **Edit Title** quick menu on the left-hand side of the dashboard page and then click anywhere on the report page to commit the change. If a custom link is required, you can set it here as well.

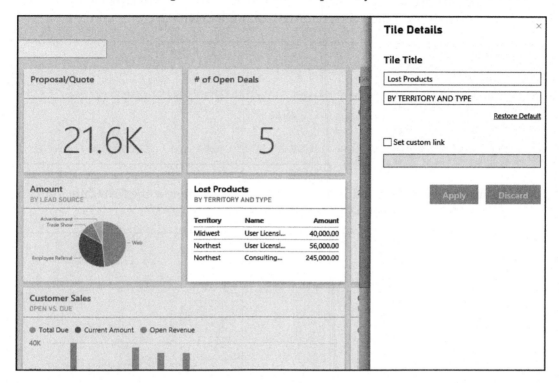

Setting up refresh schedules

Keeping the dashboard's data up to date used to be a painful process. However, now we have the configuration settings to schedule dataset refreshes in Power BI for the Office 365 site.

 Currently, Power BI does not support refresh schedules from a Power BI Designer file import, but this functionality is coming soon. For the latest information about refresh schedules, refer to https://support.powerbi.com/ knowledgebase/articles/474669-refresh-data-in-power-bi.

Let's take a look at an example of how we could schedule a refresh or manually refresh datasets:

1. Under **Datasets** in the main site window, select the fly out submenu for sales productivity and then click on **SCHEDULE REFRESH**:

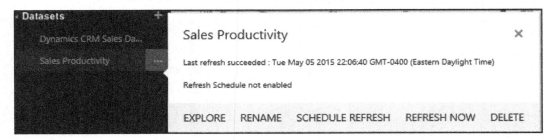

2. Once the new site window appears for **Settings**, review the **Schedule Refresh** and **Manage Data Sources** options:

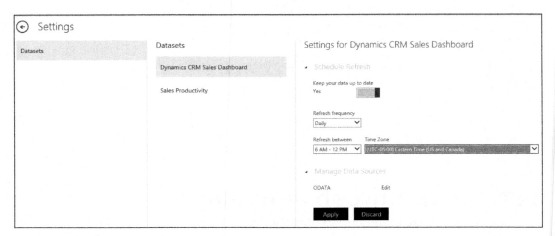

Sharing dashboards with people

Providing access to the sales productivity dashboard is now easier than ever. By simply sharing the dashboard, users can immediately invite others to start analyzing data. In order to do this, each user must have an active Office 365 user account with an e-mail address.

Let's take a look at an example of how we share the sales productivity dashboard using **Power BI for Office 365** sites:

1. In the query view window, select **Get Data** from the **Home** tab under the top menu and then select the **SQL Server** option.

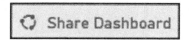

2. While in the query view window, select **Get Data** from the **Home** tab under the top menu, and select **SQL Server** option.

Summary

In this chapter, you learned how to upload and share the Power BI Designer file to the Power BI for the Office 365 site. We also looked at how to set up refreshable schedules to keep the data up to date. We saw an example of how to create and edit the reports with some of the same functionalities as the Power BI Designer, but using the site editing features.

In the next chapter, we will expand on the use of the Power BI for the Office 365 site by exploring the Q&A functionality in our dashboard. Once we understand how Q&A works, we will pin additional tiles based on the Q&A information using the sales productivity dashboard.

8
Using Power BI Q&A to Get Results

Once you deploy your sales productivity reports to Power BI for the Office 365 site, you have many different ways to analyze your data, but what if you could formulate a series of queries-based textual questions and your dashboard could show you the results you asked for?

Let's say you are the sales manager and you want to see the sales pipeline information by stage, territory, or practice, but you do not have the means to point-and-click and render the results.

The Power BI site for Office 365, using native functionality that allows written Q&A or, in the near future, spoken words, to formulate results from your dashboard is another great way to query the data.

In this chapter, you will learn how to use the Q&A functionality in the sales productivity dashboard by:

- Learning how to use the responsive Q&A functionality
- Pinning Q&A results to the sales productivity dashboard
- Sharing Q&A entries with other users
- Discussing voice to text options with the Q&A functionality

What is Power BI for Office 365 Q&A?

The Power BI for Office 365 Q&A is a feature that incorporates a natural language base to interact with data. Q&A is a great way to use your natural language to search, analyze, and report data. At its simplest, the functionality is built with the keyword search feature for your dataset tables, columns, and calculated field names, leveraging the built-in filter, sort, aggregate, group, and display data.

For example, in the **Closed Deals by Stage** chart, we could ask a question about the total amount of estimated revenue per stage and then pin the results to the sales productivity dashboard.

Asking some questions

So how do we ask Power BI a question? At the top of the Power BI for the Office 365 site page, there is an entry field for a question. The results will render a display in the form of visualizations. By entering a question, Power BI Q&A finds the chart and the table of map to represent the answer. By just typing a simple questions into the **Sales Productivity** text box, we can begin to see the power of the Q&A functionality.

Sales Productivity Share Dashboard

Ask a question about the data on this dashboard

Before you start to add some questions to the sales productivity dashboard, there are a few things to know. The Power BI for Office 365 site is available in 44 different languages.

 For more information about the languages supported by Power BI for Office 365, refer to https://support.powerbi.com/knowledgebase/articles/559626-supported-languages-for-power-bi.

When you type natural language queries with Power BI Q&A, there are only the following keyword search types that you can specify in the query:

* Columns and tables
* Data values
* Relationships
* The contextual ambiguity resolution
* Sorting

- Equality filters
- Date range filters
- Aggregation and grouping
- Explicit visualization type requests

For the sales productivity dashboard, we have already added a lot of good information from the CRM and ERP systems. Another great addition may be showing some totals or adding some direct numbers to the dashboard.

To do this, we need to use the Q&A functionality and save the results to the dashboard. Let's build a few examples for the sales productivity dashboard:

- Show total revenue qualify, develop, and propose
- Show **Count of Opportunity Open**
- Show **Lost Deals by Territory**
- Show **Number of Opportunities by Sales Stage by Name**
- Show **customer aging**

Asking the dashboard a question may be the fastest way to get results from the dashboard. Remember to pin all the results with the same method you learned in *Chapter 7, Deploy and Present Reports to the Power BI Site*. To ask your first question, follow these steps:

1. Under the Q&A textbox, enter individually **Total Qualify**, **Total Qualify Develop**, and **Total Qualify Propose** to show the total amounts of each **Sale Stage**:

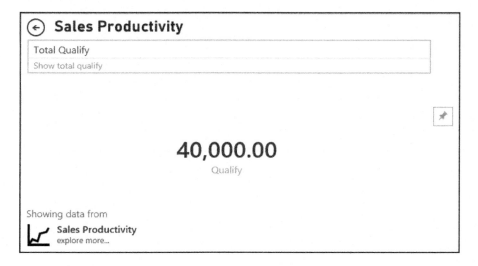

2. Pin () the results to the main **Sales Productivity** dashboard.

3. Under the Q&A textbox, enter **Count of Opportunity Open** to show the total count of open opportunities:

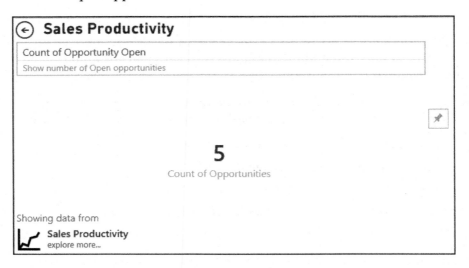

4. Pin () the results to the main sales productivity dashboard.

5. Under the Q&A textbox, enter **Lost Deals by Territory that are named User Licencing** to show the lost user licencing deals lost:

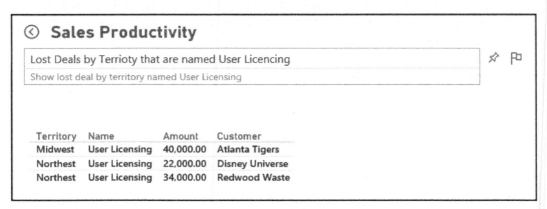

6. Repeat the step and enter **Show Lost Deals by Territory that are named Consulting Services** to show the lost consulting deals.

7. Pin (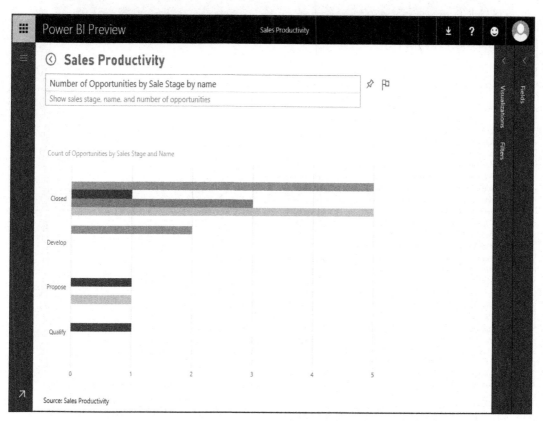) the results to the main sales productivity dashboard.

8. Moving on, enter **Number of Opportunities by Sale Stage by name** to show a graphical horizontal bar chart:

9. Pin ( ) the results to the main sales productivity dashboard.

Now that we have new charts and tables added to our sales productivity dashboard page based on the simple Q&A functionality, let's spice it up a little and see whether we can pull some informative ERP information for our customer.

Let's show the **customer aging** data that we now have access to after joining the CRM and ERP datasets. Here is what we do:

1. Under the Q&A textbox, enter **customer aging** to all customers that match in CRM with terms, class, and aging buckets:

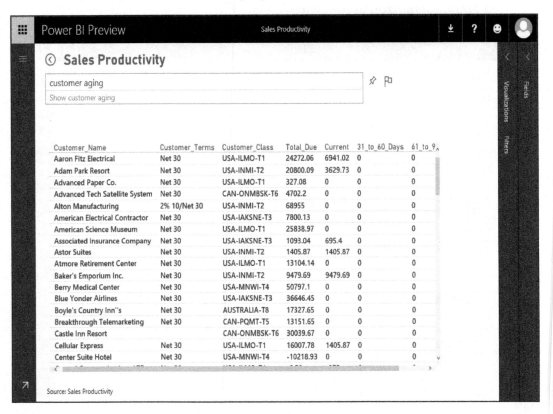

2. Pin ( ) the results to the main sales productivity dashboard.

Pinning the results to the dashboard

Pinning results and/or reports to a dashboard in Power BI for Office 365 site offers a very flexible way to view multiple angles of data in one location. Any time you hover over a visualization, the pinning icon will show.

For the most updated list of all the supported pinnable dashboards, refer to the Power BI link at `https://support.powerbi.com/knowledgebase/articles/611046-visualizations-that-can-be-pinned-to-a-dashboard`.

When you select the pinned icon (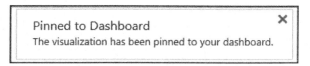), it may or may not pin the item to the main dashboard based on whether it is supported yet. If an item is pinned successfully, it will alert you with a popup window in the top-right corner of Power BI for the Office 365 site page.

Here is an example of this window:

> Pinned to Dashboard ✕
> The visualization has been pinned to your dashboard.

After pinning each of the preceding Q&A result sets, we now need to move the tiles and adjust the titles.

Here is example of how you do this for the sales productivity dashboard:

1. Using the methods from *Chapter 7*, *Deploy and Present Reports to the Power BI Site*, drag **Total Qualify**, **Total Qualify Develop**, **Total Qualify Propose**, and **Count of Opportunities**.

2. Rename the tiles to **Qualification**, **Development**, **Proposal/Quote**, and **# of Open Deals**.

3. Review the final sales productivity dashboard and remove any unneeded pinned items.

Sales Productivity Dashboard in Office 365 Power BI sites

Sharing your results on the fly

Using the Q&A functionality in Power BI for Office 365 sites opens the door to a world of future possibilities. Posting dashboards to a website is the one feature that has the potential to make it easy for anyone to perform business intelligence, for example, the sales manager who asks for a weekly sales report may just not have to ask for it anymore. We can provide him with a straightforward self-served business intelligence method.

A great way to get that sales manager and others involved immediately is to simply e-mail them the Q&A result page. Sending them something prebuilt on real-time data allows them to test scenarios until they get comfortable with the Q&A feature.

Here is a quick way to provide someone access to the exact Q&A result you have created:

1. In the Power BI Q&A, enter a question and review the results.
2. While still in Power BI for the Office 365 site, copy the URL and send it to any other users. When a user opens the URL, they are presented with the exact same result view.
3. Once a user receives the URL, he can begin using the Q&A result page and manipulating the data based on his requirements.

Voice to text options

Wouldn't it be nice to just ask the question to Power BI for the Office 365 site to render the reporting data you are looking for? In the near future, Microsoft's Power BI team will take the next steps to integrate Cortana and so on with this Q&A functionality so that users can ask questions from the sales productivity datasets using a phone or microphone.

Imagine the power of being able to tell users to verbally "Ask questions of your data". This type of functionality is available with the integrated speech to text software. A user can click on the Q&A box and start asking the question. In the future, this type of integration will be seamless in Power BI.

Summary

In this chapter, you learned how to use the responsive Q&A feature in Power BI for Office 365. We formulated a few questions and pinned the results to the sales productivity dashboard. You also learned how to quickly share the Q&A results with other users and the possible future functionalities involving voice to text.

In the next chapter, we will see examples of how we can display the sales productivity reports within Dynamics CRM 2015.

9
Extending the Sales Productivity Dashboard within Dynamics CRM 2015

Finally, let's say a sales manager logged in to Dynamics CRM and wanted to see the same sales pipeline information by **Stage**, **Territory**, or **Practice**, which he has been looking at in the Power BI for Office 365 sites, but does not want to leave Dynamics CRM.

In this chapter, we will show you various options of how to access sales productivity dashboards and reports from Dynamics CRM with a simple HTML page and menu items from the main navigational section. We will use a published web resource that we loaded to our Dynamics CRM instance, linking us to the Power BI for the Office 365 sales productivity dashboards and reports. We will perform this by:

- Learning how to configure the Dynamics CRM solution
- Adding a HTML menu web page with a web resource to Dynamics CRM that links to the Power BI sales productivity dashboards and reports
- Reviewing issues with OOTB IFrames and future additions to Dynamics CRM with Power BI

 Out-Of-The-Box (OOTB), there is no way to embed a Power BI into Dynamics CRM at the moment. In the future, the Power BI development team will prepare to add features that will allow this to work. For now, we will build the functionality with a little custom code.

Configuring Internet Explorer

Before we start to embed the sales productivity dashboard and report menu page in Dynamics CRM, we first need to adjust some Internet Explorer settings.

Here is what we do:

1. In Internet Explorer, navigate to **Internet Options** | **Security**, select **Trusted Sites** and then **Sites**:

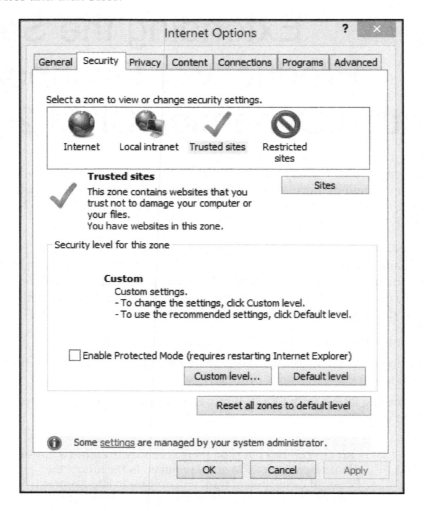

2. Add the Dynamics CRM and Power BI for the Office 365 site to the trusted zone:

3. Once you have the sites added to the trusted zone, select the **Custom level** button from the **Security** tab, set the option to **Enable** for **Display mixed content**, and restart IE:

Configuring the web resource

Now that we have our browser environment configured, we are ready to create a *new* Dynamics CRM solution to add the HTML menu page in order to access the Power BI sales productivity dashboard within Dynamics CRM. To deploy a solution with a custom HTML web page in Dynamics CRM, we need to use a web resource.

 The web resource is usually added to a unique Dynamics CRM solution. It represents files that can be used to extend the Microsoft Dynamics CRM web application, such as HTML files, JavaScript, and Silverlight applications. Once published, these web resources will become a part of the Dynamics CRM instance in form customizations, the Sitemap, or the application ribbon. These become available for use by using the URL syntax. For this chapter, a sample web resource has been created and is available for download at `https://www.dropbox.com/s/950gozygjihm5z6/power_bi_menu.html?dl=0`

For more information about web resources, refer to

`https://msdn.microsoft.com/en-us/library/gg309473.aspx`

Once you have the web resource file downloaded, you need to update the actual navigational link entries in the file sections to match your instance of the Power BI dashboards and reports. This is a fairly easy process, but it requires the specific **Global Unique Identifier (GUID)** for your Power BI for the Office 365 site dashboards and reports. Here is how we do it:

1. From your browser, open your Power BI sales productivity dashboard and copy the GUID links from the URL.

2. Now, open the downloaded web resource file with notepad, find and replace each section in the highlighted area, as shown in the following code, with the GUIDs you just copied, replacing them with your specific Power BI Instance information. Then, save and close the file:

```
<h1>Power BI Links</h1>
  <div style="padding-left: 20px; padding-right: 5px;
padding-top: 5px; padding-bottom: 5px;">
    <h2>Dashboards</h2>
    <div style="padding-left: 20px; padding-right: 5px;">
      <h3><a class="ms-crm-List-Link"
href="https://app.powerbi.com/groups/me/dashboards/74386daa-
2a62-42a3-8bfc-f40f2f75ab72" target="Power BI">Sales
Productivity Dashboard</a></h3>
```

```
      </div>
    </div>
    <div style="padding-left: 20px; padding-right: 5px;
  padding-top: 5px; padding-bottom: 5px;">
      <h2>Reports</h2>
      <div style="padding-left: 50px; padding-right: 5px;">
        <h3><a class="ms-crm-List-Link"
  href="https://app.powerbi.com/groups/me/reports/43fef548-
  f340-4caa-b747-e58fe7b5a117" target="Power BI">Sales
  Productivity Report</a></h3>
```

Now that we have our specific GUIDs added to the HTML file, we can create and publish a Dynamics CRM solution with a web resource for the HTML menu web page to our current instance.

Creating the Dynamics CRM solution

While in Dynamics CRM, we need to create a new solution with the HTML menu page web resource to access the Power BI dashboards and reports. To start, we will create a new solution just for the Power BI dashboard and report custom web page.

Here is how we will create the new Dynamics CRM solution:

1. While in Dynamics CRM, navigate to **SETTINGS | Solutions** and select **New** from the top submenu bar under **All Solutions**:

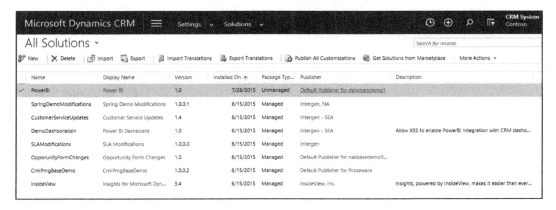

2. Once the **New Solution** form opens, name your solution and save it. In this example, I got really creative and named the dashboard as **Power BI**. How original, right?

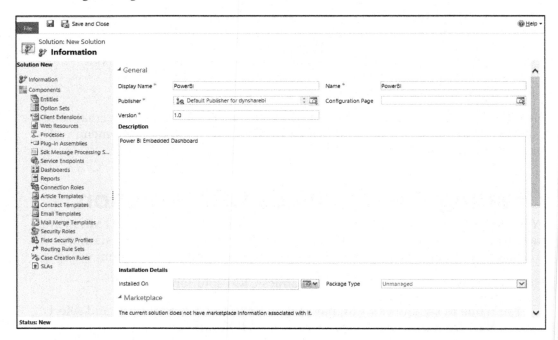

3. Now, select **Web Resources** from the left-hand side menu and add a new web resource for our HTML page:

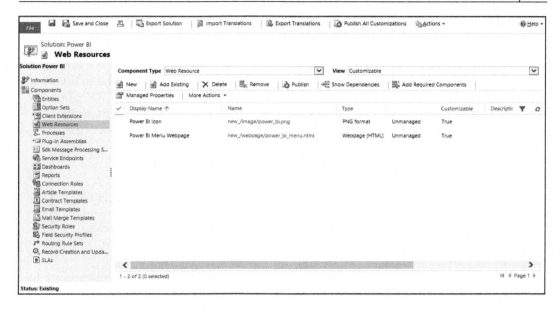

4. Enter the information for **Web Resource: Power BI Menu Webpage**, set the **Type** to **Webpage (HTML)**, and upload the HTML file that you downloaded:

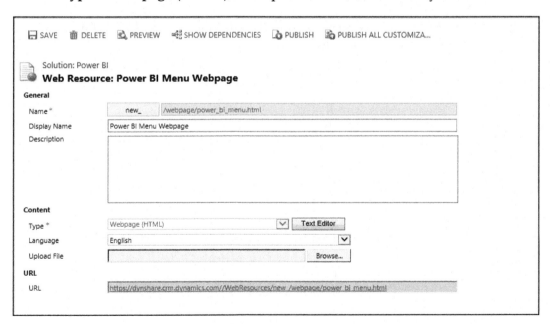

5. After the web resource is added to **Solution**, select **SAVE** and **PUBLISH ALL CUSTOMIZATIONS**.

Updating the Sitemap

Now that you have a new solution, we need to add navigational links to Dynamics CRM to point to the HTML menu web page so that we can easily find it. We can do this by updating the Dynamics CRM Sitemap. The Sitemap is basically the main layout of the Dynamics CRM navigation and menu links. Having a Dynamics CRM Sitemap ready to link to the Power BI menu web page with links to the sales productivity dashboard and reports should be pretty easy if we have the right to do so.

 Adding any type of external site links to Dynamics CRM can always be a challenge. Until the native Power BI IFrame functionality is available in Dynamics CRM, there will always be environmental concerns involving operations systems, browsers, and the user security. You may have to do a little trial and error to get the Power BI dashboard working with Dynamics CRM.

To adjust the Sitemap we follow the same steps as we did to add a Web Resource to the Solution, but instead, this time we export and edit the solution with the Sitemap from Dynamics CRM. Here is how we do it:

1. While in Dynamics CRM, navigate to **SETTINGS | Solutions** and open the Power BI solution.

2. Navigate to **Client Extensions** from the left-hand side **Solution Power BI** menu and select **Add Existing | Site Map**:

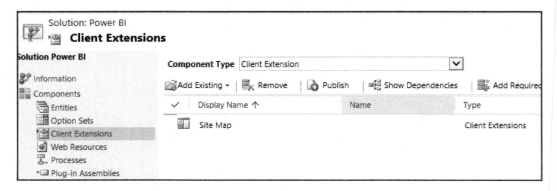

3. Save and export the **PowerBI** solution as an **Unmanaged** type.

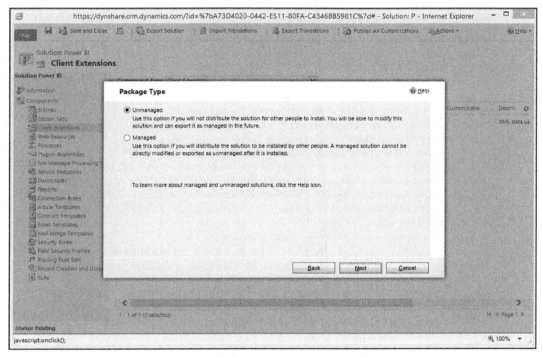

The Unmanaged solution

4. Once the file is downloaded to a file named `PowerBI_1_0.zip`, open the `customizations.xml` file using notepad that is in the `.zip` file:

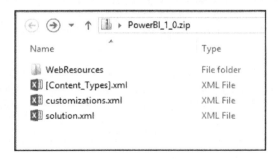

5. With the file open in the text format, find MyWork Group anywhere in the Sitemap and add a new SubArea for the Power BI menu web page. For this book, we will use the following example:

```
<Group Id="MyWork" ResourceId="Group_MyWork"
DescriptionResourceId="My_Work_Description"
IntroducedVersion="7.0.0.0">
        <SubArea Id="nav_dashboards"
ResourceId="Homepage_Dashboards"
DescriptionResourceId="Dashboards_Description"
Icon="/_imgs/area/18_home.gif"
Url="/workplace/home_dashboards.aspx"
GetStartedPanePath="Dashboards_Web_User_Visor.html"
GetStartedPanePathAdmin="Dashboards_Web_Admin_Visor.html"
GetStartedPanePathOutlook="Dashboards_Outlook_User_Visor.html"
GetStartedPanePathAdminOutlook="Dashboards_Outlook_Admin_Visor.htm
l" DefaultDashboard="B46AEB74-BF0C-44FB-8158-9575588D1B57"
IntroducedVersion="7.0.0.0" />
        <SubArea Id="nav_activities"
DescriptionResourceId="Activities_SubArea_Description"
Url="/_root/homepage.aspx?etc=4200" Entity="activitypointer"
GetStartedPanePath="Activities_Web_User_Visor.html"
GetStartedPanePathAdmin="Activities_Web_Admin_Visor.html"
GetStartedPanePathOutlook="Activities_Outlook_User_Visor.html"
GetStartedPanePathAdminOutlook="Activities_Outlook_Admin_Visor.htm
l" IntroducedVersion="7.0.0.0" />
        <SubArea
GetStartedPanePath="Dashboards_Web_User_Visor.html"
GetStartedPanePathAdmin="Dashboards_Web_Admin_Visor.html"
GetStartedPanePathAdminOutlook="Dashboards_Outlook_Admin_Visor.htm
l" GetStartedPanePathOutlook="Dashboards_Outlook_User_Visor.html"
Icon="$webresource:new_/image/power_bi.png" Id="PowerBI"
Url="$webresource:new_/webpage/power_bi_menu.html" Title="PowerBI"
AvailableOffline="false" PassParams="false" Client="Web" />
        </Group>
```

6. To add a custom icon to the menu link, load another web resource with a type of icon and update the following entry in the preceding sitemap example. For this chapter, I have reused the default dashboard: Icon, but you could easily add a custom Power BI Icon, as shown in the following code

```
Icon="$webresource:new_/image/power_bi.png" Id="PowerBI
```

7. Finally, add the updated `customizations.xml` file back to the `PowerBI_1_0.zip` file, import the solution back to the Dynamics CRM solution, and navigate to the Power BI menu item, as shown in the following code:

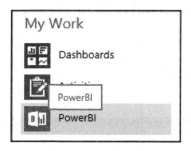

8. Once the `PowerBI_1_0.zip` file is uploaded, publish the PowerBI solution, refresh the web browser, navigate to the menu web page, and select an item link to open the Power BI dashboard or report:

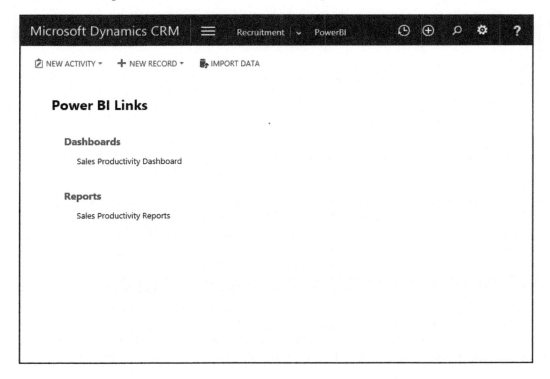

Why not use an IFrame?

Although it is most certainly true that the most ideal way to show Power BI for the Office 365 site dashboard and/or report should be straight from the IFrame in Dynamics CRM, just like the way Power View add-in from Excel uploaded to SharePoint does, this is not possible with the Power BI site for Office 365 at the moment because Power BI will not allow itself to be loaded into IFrames due to security reasons. If you attempt to add the Power BI for Office 365 dashboard and report link to IFrame using the properties form, you will be prompted with an unresponsive **Sign In** page:

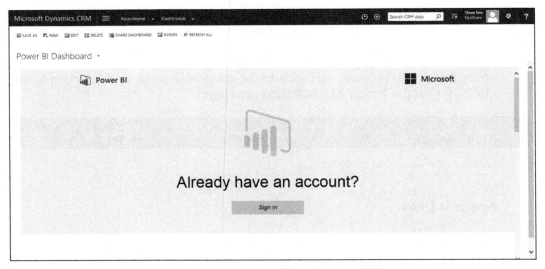

The Power BI site Sign In from Dynamics CRM

Although there may be possible custom-developed solutions to get around presenting the dashboards in Dynamics CRM, it would include the advanced implementation configuration that we will not focus on in this book.

What is coming in the near future?

As Power BI continues to evolve, there will be more natively integrated points for Dynamics CRM. One of these points is to make the Power BI information accessible to cut/paste/embed to other areas in Dynamics CRM. Although these features are not yet available, it will be included with the general availability version launch of Power BI.

Using an OOTB IFrame to visualize the dashboards just as you do to the native Dynamics CRM dashboards would be a widely popular method in the Dynamics CRM community and would make Dynamics CRM advanced reporting more seamless to the end user. A hint would be that it might be coming to Dynamics CRM soon.

Summary

In this chapter, you learned how to add a new Dynamics CRM solution to embed a menu web page to access the Power BI sales productivity dashboard in Dynamics CRM. You also learned how to configure the Dynamics CRM dashboard and review the future native functionality, which is coming soon for Dynamics CRM.

In the next chapter, we will look at examples of how we can take the sales productivity reports mobile with tablets and phones.

10
Extend Your Dashboards to Mobile Apps

Mobile apps are the wave of the future and are becoming the easiest way to access data. Whether it's your tablet or mobile phone, always having access to your company's information is the only way to go.

Let's say you are the sales manager and want to see the sales pipeline information, but you do not have any means to do so. Maybe, you are traveling and do not have immediate access to a computer, but need to quickly query some data.

The answers are in the Power BI app. Power BI has a native app for Windows and iOS. This works with both tablets and phones. In this chapter, you will learn how to present the sales productivity dashboard using these apps:

- Getting the Power BI app
- Deploying the Power BI app for Surface
- Deploying the Power BI app for iOS

Getting the Power BI app

The fastest way to load the Power BI app is to navigate to the store on the device and download it. Another way is to navigate to the Power BI website and use the link at `http://powerbi.microsoft.com/downloads`.

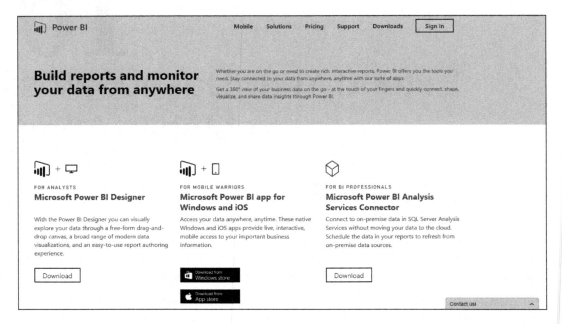

Once the app is loaded on a device, we need to configure the settings based on a specific Power BI instance in Office 365. Let's install and configure the Power BI app and connect to our sales productivity dashboard.

Using the Surface app

One of the most popular devices today is Microsoft Surface. One of the main reasons why it is so popular is the business apps available for download in the Microsoft Store. One of these is the Power BI app that is designed to work natively with Microsoft Surface and Windows OS. It's no surprise that Microsoft would create a device that is made for apps, such as Power BI and Dynamics CRM 2015. Why wouldn't a Microsoft product play well with another Microsoft product?

Here is how we get working on Microsoft Surface and Windows Phone:

1. Navigate to the Windows Store on Microsoft Surface and install the app:

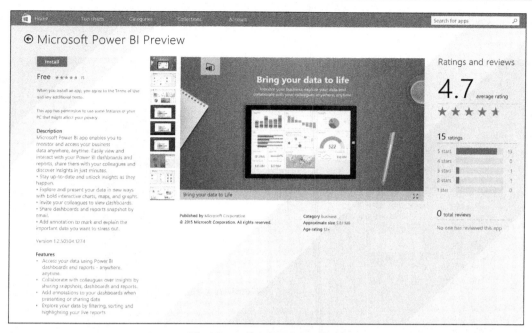

The Microsoft Power BI Preview

2. Locate the installed app under the Windows **Apps by name** screen:

The installed apps

3. Select the app and then sign in to your service with your Power BI instance username and password:

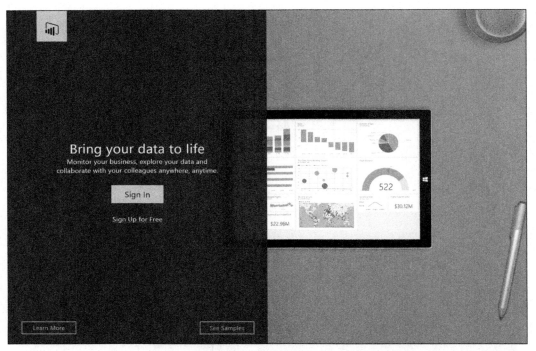

The sign in screen

4. To log in to the Power BI app, select the **Let's Get Started** button at the top of the screen to open the Power BI app.

5. Once the Power BI app is open, you will see links to **Dashboards**, **Reports**, and **Sample Dashboards**. Select the **Sales Productivity** tab under **Dashboards** to open the sales productivity dashboard:

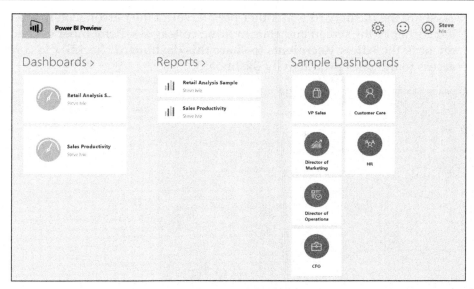

The Power BI Preview interface

6. The **Sales Productivity** dashboard will have the same look and feel as the Power BI for the Office 365 website version:

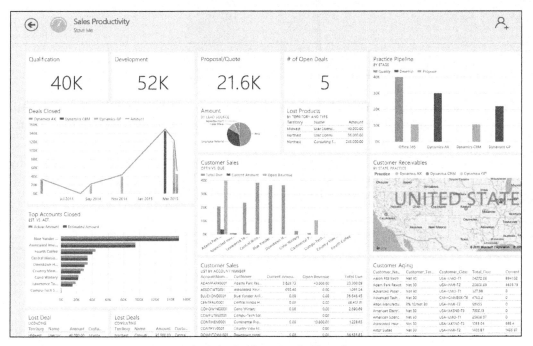

The Sales Productivity dashboard

7. To share the dashboard with other people, select the person icon in the top-left corner of the screen and start inviting colleagues. Remember to check or uncheck the **Allow Recipients to share this dashboard** checkbox to control access to the sales productivity dashboard:

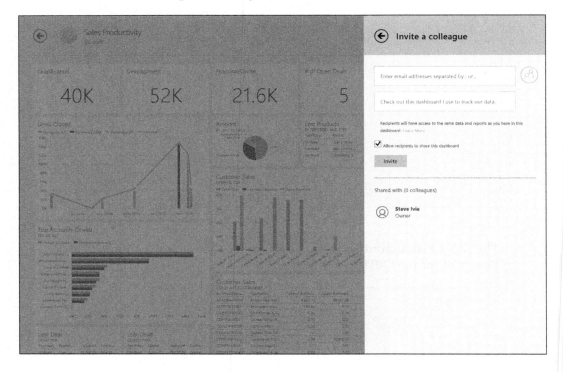

8. To access the reports, select a panel on the main dashboard just as you would on the Power BI for the Office 365 site. Once the panel is selected, the report will be displayed.

9. The Power BI app reports are a bit more interactive with a touch-enabled line identifier. Move the line through the different bars in the graph to see the actual values in the top-left corner of the report.

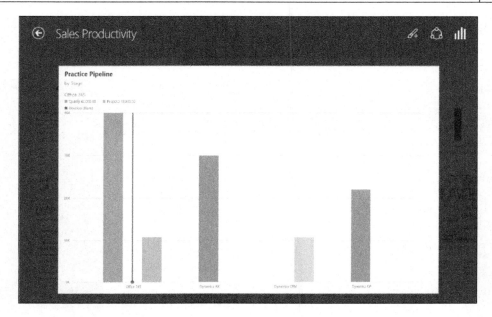

10. The Power BI app reports also include the **Annotate** functionality to mark the actual report in the dashboard. Click on the paintbrush icon located in the top-right corner of the report screen to see the options available to add annotations:

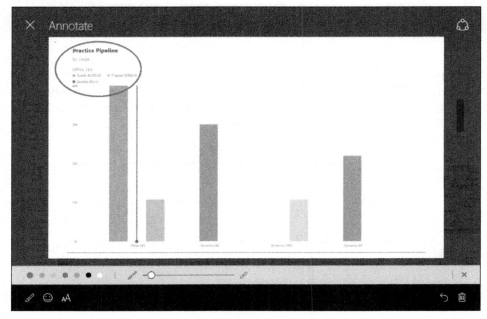

Practice Pipeline Report with Annotate

11. Now that you have added some annotations in the report, share it via **Mail**, **OneNote**, or a social feed—such as Twitter—by clicking on **Share** in the top-right corner of the report screen:

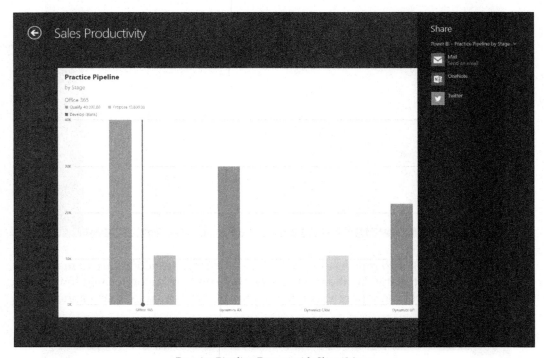

Practice Pipeline Report with Share Menu

There are quite a few options that you can leverage to access the sales productivity dashboard in the Power BI app, but what if you do not use a Windows device? What if you use an iPhone or an iPad? Let's take a look at how we can install and configure the Power BI app for iOS.

Using the iOS app

Most business users who are not using Microsoft Surface or Windows Phone are using the ever so popular iPad and iPhone. The iPad runs the iOS operating system, and Power BI has an app specifically for it. The Power BI app for iOS has a little different look and feel, but it is built with the same functionality, and it works just as well.

Here is how we get the Power BI app working on an iOS device, such as iPad and iPhone:

1. Navigate to the App Store on the iPad or iPhone and install the Microsoft Power BI Preview app:

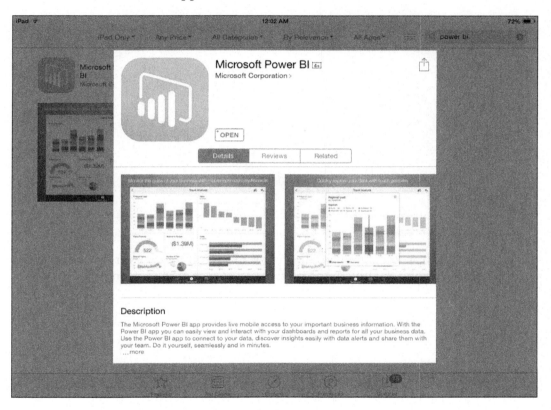

2. After the installation is complete, locate the app on the homescreen.

The Power BI app is seen in the bottom-right (third row) on your mobile interface

3. Select the app and sign in to the Power BI instance with your username and password with the link in the bottom-left corner of the screen:

4. Once the Power BI app is open, you will see various links to the sales productivity dashboard and options at the bottom of the screen for **Favorites**, **Reports**, **Alerts**, and **Settings**. Select the **Sales Productivity** panel to open the sales productivity dashboard:

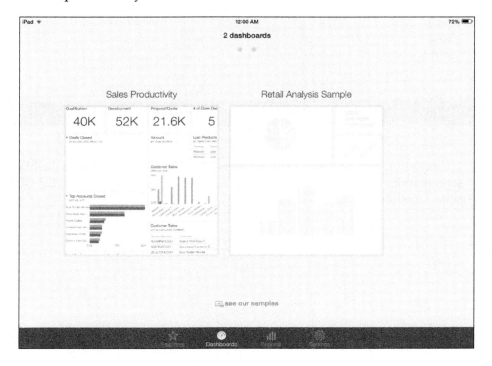

5. Again, the sales productivity dashboard will have the same look and feel as the Power BI for the Office 365 website version. Using the **Favorites** icon located at the bottom of the dashboard screen, we can pin a report to the main screen for faster access:

The Sales Productivity dashboard as seen on your mobile app

6. To access the reports, select the **Reports** icon at the bottom of the dashboard screen. Once the panel is selected, the report will be displayed on top of the actual dashboard:

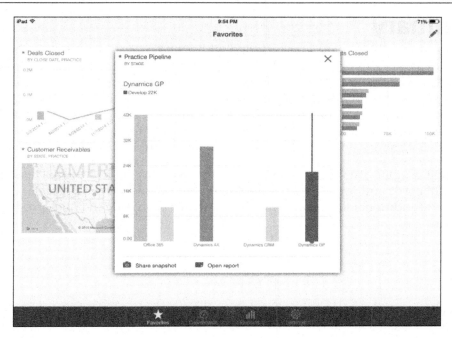

7. Using the iOS app, we can **Mail**, **Facebook**, **Save Image**, **Assign to Contact**, **Copy**, or **Print** by selecting the pencil icon in the top-right corner of the screen:

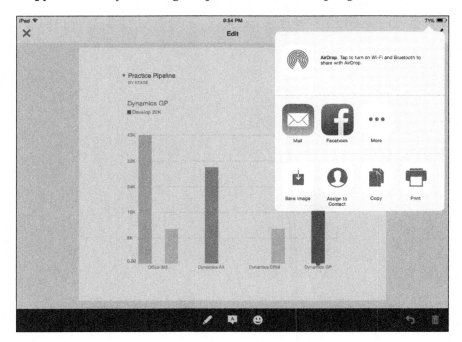

Summary

There are many different options included with each Power BI app. In this chapter, we only explored a few examples of the Windows and iOS app, but the Android app is now also available. You learned how to install and configure the core functionality and use and share individual dashboards and reports. We also discovered that we cannot build and deploy the Power BI reports with mobile apps, such as the web client. The mobile version of the Power BI app is mostly used to quickly display the data in visualizations and drill down the most important information.

In the next chapter, we will see examples of how we can add additional Dynamics 2015 dashboards and reports fast by deploying the Sales Manager template. We will also review additional templates available to deploy alongside the sales productivity dashboard.

11
Starting with the Built-in Dashboard Templates

Wouldn't it be nice if we could just start with a good sales dashboard template like the ones that come out of the box with Dynamics CRM 2015 dashboards?

Well, you can. Power BI for Office 365 sites include native connectors that load the sales management dashboard for Dynamics CRM 2015. This dashboard is loaded with prebuilt reports and datasets around the Sales Pipeline Management.

Along with the Dynamics CRM 2015 sales manager template, there are also templates for marketing and service that can be added.

In this chapter, you will learn how to get started with the Dynamics CRM 2015 dashboard templates by doing the following:

- Loading the sales manager dashboard
- Exploring future dashboards for marketing and service

Loading the sales manager dashboard

Loading the Dynamics CRM 2015 sales manager template is as simple as connecting to the CRM site. Once you connect to Dynamics CRM 2015 with the connector, the data will be loaded to the Power BI for the Office 365 site. This is simple.

Here is how it is done:

1. In Power BI for Office 365, select the **Get Data** link in the bottom-left corner of the window. Once the **Get Data** selection appears, under **Content Pack Library**, choose **Services**:

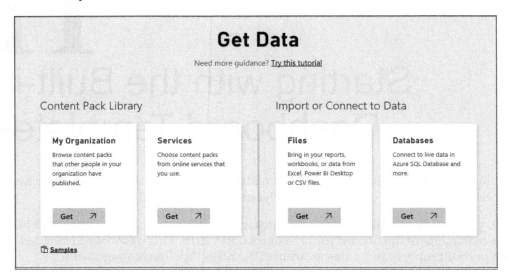

2. Select the connection option for **Microsoft Dynamics CRM** and then click on **Connect**:

3. Using the same steps as in *Chapter 1, Getting Dynamics CRM 2015 Data into Power BI,* add the OData Service URL to the **Configure Dynamics CRM Sales** window and click on **Next**:

4. Once prompted for **Authentication Method** on the **Configure Dynamics CRM Sales** window, select **oAuth2**:

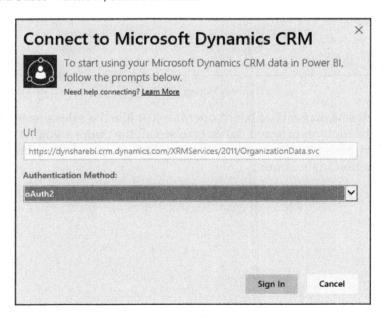

5. The **Sales Manager** dashboard will begin to load. Wait until each pane shows the data:

The Sales Manager Dashboard

6. The **Sales Manager** dashboard operates just like the sales productivity. Click through reports and datasets to see all the options you have to query the data. Select the **Revenue by Owner** chart to review the additional information in the report.

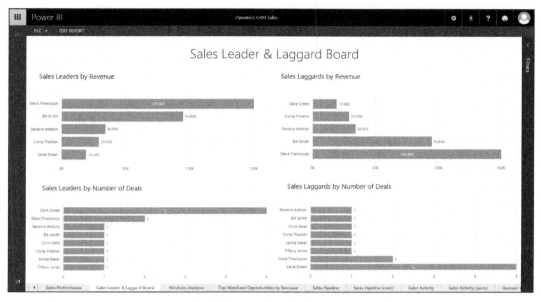

Additional information available in the report

What's coming next?

Power BI for Office 365 and the Power BI Designer are constantly being updated to fit the needs of its user's base. Every month, there are updates that can include new application or database templates. For Dynamics CRM 2015, in the near future, there will be additional dashboards for marketing and case management reporting.

As the Power BI product matures, there will surely be more and more templates added to the options that you can connect to. As shown in *Chapter 6, Adding ERP Data*, adding additional data sources will give us the ability to join and merge data so that we can gain deeper insights into the organization.

Currently, some of the more commonly - used data sources that are integrated into Dynamics CRM 2015 include the following:

- Dynamics marketing
- Marketo
- Twilio
- Google Analytics
- SQL Server Analysis services
- Visual Studio Online
- The Azure SQL database

Summary

In this chapter, we reviewed a quicker way to get started with Power BI and Dynamics CRM 2015 with the native sales manager template. We also discussed the rapid release of new enhancements and templates as the Power BI application grows.

We looked at how to build a sales productivity dashboard from scratch with Dynamics CRM and Power BI. Along the way, we explored a number of different ways to construct and shape our data so that we can build reports and dashboards for a sales organization. Power BI has a few different tools and delivery options, including Designer, Officer 365 sites, and apps. Allowing end users the option of connecting Power BI to Dynamics CRM and additional sources opens a whole new world to self-served business intelligence. This chapter provided you some insights into how to use this powerful tool, and showed you how to get started with Dynamics CRM 2015 and Power BI.

Now, give it a try and see what you discover. I hope that you have found a brand new insight into your organization, no matter what level you are at.

Index

A

amounts
  formatting 35, 36

C

cards 66-69
charts 68, 69
cloud
  ERP data, accessing from 98-100
cluster column chart 59-61
clustered bar chart 61-63
column data types
  preparing 25-27
column filter 76, 77
columns
  renaming 36-39
column values
  filtering 28, 29
customer aging
  joining 93, 94
  script 89

D

dashboard
  pinnable dashboards, URL 121
  Power BI, URL 102
  results, pinning to Power BI for
    Office 365 120-122
  sharing, with people 113
  visualizations, reporting 108, 109
data
  filtering 72
  filters, adding 76
  getting 91, 92

data clarity
  enhancing 71
data, filtering
  drill down 73, 74
  fly-out 73
  sort 75
datasets
  combining 29-32
  querying process 21, 22
  relationships, planning 20, 21
  renaming 36-39
data sources 157
dates
  formatting 35, 36
DateTime filter 77-79
drill-down 73, 74
Dynamics CRM 2015
  about 1, 2
  datasets 20
  new solution, creating 129-131
Dynamics CRM 2015 Online
  adding 3
  OData connection, finding 5
  sample data, importing 5
  user access, providing 4
Dynamics CRM, connecting to
  about 11
  data, accessing 12, 13
  data, loading 14
  data, querying 15, 16
  requisites, checking 11
Dynamics GP
  customer aging script 89-91
  deployment 88
  URL 91

E

ERP data
  accessing, from cloud 98-100

F

fields
  calculating 46-48
file
  uploading, to Power BI site 103-105
filled map 63-66
filters
  adding, to data 76
  column filter 76, 77
  DateTime filter 77-79
  page filters, using 82-84
  report filters 79
  visualization filters 80-82
fly-out 73

G

Global Unique Identifier (GUID) 128

I

IFrame
  using 136
Internet Explorer
  configuring 126, 127
Internet-facing deployment (IFD) 3
iOS app
  using 147
iOS device
  Power BI app, using 147-151

L

list values
  replacing 32-34

O

OData connection
  finding 5, 6

OData (REST) authentication methods
  Anonymous 10
  Basic 11
  marketplace key 11
  Organizational account 11
  reviewing 10
  Web API 11
  Windows 10
Office 365
  setting up 2
  URL 2
Office 365 site
  Power BI, setting up 7
Out-Of-The-Box (OOTB) 125

P

page filters
  using 82-84
pie chart 54-56
pivot columns 45, 46
Power BI
  for Office 365 157
  for Office 365 site 101, 102
  future enhancements 136, 137
  pricing, URL 101
  setting up, for Office 365 site 7
  URL 7
Power BI app
  about 140
  downloading 140
  URL 140
  using, on iOS device 147-151
Power BI Designer
  about 8
  installing 8, 9
Power BI, for Office 365
  languages, URL 116
  Q&A 116
  questions, asking 116-120
  results, pinning to dashboard 120-122
  results, sharing 122
  voice to text options 123
Power BI Personal Gateway
  URL 98

Power BI site
file, uploading 103-105
reports, editing within 105-108
power query syntax
URL 48

R

refresh schedules
setting up 111, 112
URL 111
report
building 95-97
editing, within Power BI site 105-108
starting 50-52
report filters
about 79
interacting with 79
rows
grouping 43-45

S

sales manager dashboard
loading 153-156
sales productivity dashboards, accessing
Dynamics CRM solution, creating 129-131
IFrame, using 136
Internet Explorer, configuring 126, 127
Sitemap, updating 132-135
web resource, configuring 128
Sitemap
updating 132-135
slicers
adding 84-86
sort 75
SQL Server
URL 88
stacked combo chart
about 52
building 53, 54
summary information 42, 43
Surface app
using 140-146

T

table 57, 58
tile
pin at 109
renaming 110

U

unused columns
removing 22-25

V

visualization filters 80-82
visualizations
reporting, to dashboard 108, 109
URL 50

W

web resource
configuring 128
reference link 128

Thank you for buying
Building Dynamics CRM 2015 Dashboards with Power BI

About Packt Publishing

Packt, pronounced 'packed', published its first book, *Mastering phpMyAdmin for Effective MySQL Management*, in April 2004, and subsequently continued to specialize in publishing highly focused books on specific technologies and solutions.

Our books and publications share the experiences of your fellow IT professionals in adapting and customizing today's systems, applications, and frameworks. Our solution-based books give you the knowledge and power to customize the software and technologies you're using to get the job done. Packt books are more specific and less general than the IT books you have seen in the past. Our unique business model allows us to bring you more focused information, giving you more of what you need to know, and less of what you don't.

Packt is a modern yet unique publishing company that focuses on producing quality, cutting-edge books for communities of developers, administrators, and newbies alike. For more information, please visit our website at www.packtpub.com.

About Packt Enterprise

In 2010, Packt launched two new brands, Packt Enterprise and Packt Open Source, in order to continue its focus on specialization. This book is part of the Packt Enterprise brand, home to books published on enterprise software – software created by major vendors, including (but not limited to) IBM, Microsoft, and Oracle, often for use in other corporations. Its titles will offer information relevant to a range of users of this software, including administrators, developers, architects, and end users.

Writing for Packt

We welcome all inquiries from people who are interested in authoring. Book proposals should be sent to author@packtpub.com. If your book idea is still at an early stage and you would like to discuss it first before writing a formal book proposal, then please contact us; one of our commissioning editors will get in touch with you.

We're not just looking for published authors; if you have strong technical skills but no writing experience, our experienced editors can help you develop a writing career, or simply get some additional reward for your expertise.

Microsoft Dynamics CRM Customization Essentials

ISBN: 978-1-78439-784-5   Paperback: 238 pages

Use a no-code approach to create powerful business solutions using Dynamics CRM 2015

1. Master the skills necessary to customize your system using the wizard driven capabilities of Dynamics CRM platform.

2. Use Business rules and flows to enforce and visually enhance the user experience.

3. A no-code approach to speed up the full range of Dynamics CRM features.

Microsoft Tabular Modeling Cookbook

ISBN: 978-1-78217-088-4   Paperback: 320 pages

Over 50 tips and tricks for analytical modeling using Business Intelligence Semantic Models with SQL Server 2012 and PowerPivot

1. Develop tabular models for personal use.

2. Learn about the modeling techniques which are required to overcome commonly encountered problems and master advanced modeling scenarios.

3. Understand the techniques required to promote personal models to corporate enterprise environments and manage the models in a corporate environment.

4. Learn tips and tricks for querying tabular models and learn how to access the data within them for dynamic reporting including the development of interactive workbooks.

Please check **www.PacktPub.com** for information on our titles